MW01126952

David Gerrelli is a global director of technology with practical experience in the fields of innovation, data science, emerging technologies, and global enterprise platforms. With new and emerging technologies, a large part of David's role is research and development. Winning national awards for digital innovation in Australia, David started life in the rolling hills of Surrey, South England. From there, David worked in Sydney, Australia for six years before eventually moving to the sunny southern city of Dallas, Texas.

Having had brushes with death through disease and addiction in David's early years, he became obsessed with what would await him once he drew his final breath. Decades later, David would apply his 25+ years of experience working in a field steeped in logic and science and apply these skills to years of research in the field of Near-Death Experiences. The research, tainted by David's own guilt, would take on a life of its own, revealing a dark and sinister aspect of this surprisingly common phenomenon.

What started as a journey of light would lead David down a path to the very depths of Hell. The author's rollercoaster of fear and horror would find grounding in the universal concepts of reason, science, and logic. David would apply his decades of experience within data science and analytics to cross-reference thousands of witness accounts into cohesive observations and logical conclusions, without the bias of religion or personal belief.

David studied this field and wrote this book with an open mind, and he hopes you will join him on this journey with the same open mind and childlike curiosity.

This book is dedicated to my family. To my youngest son who has had to grow beyond his years yet makes me proud with every breath I draw.

To my always loving mother Linda, my kind father Clive, my selfless oldest brother Clive Robert, my stoic and strong Tony, and my brave and courageous Juliette.

To my long-since passed Nanny Iris, a shining light within the darkness of her own grief. I think of her often and will see her again.

To my eldest son whom I eagerly await.

To all those that fear death, ponder life's meaning and seek love over judgement.

David Gerrelli

HOW TO ESCAPE FROM HELL

STUDIES & INTERPRETATIONS OF THE AFTERLIFE

AUSTIN MACAULEY PUBLISHERS™
LONDON • CAMBRIDGE • NEW YORK • SHARJAH

A CIP catalogue record for this title is available from the British Library.

ISBN 9781398446922 (Paperback)
ISBN 9781398446939 (Hardback)
ISBN 9781398446946 (ePub e-book)

www.austinmacauley.com

First Published 2022
Austin Macauley Publishers Ltd®
1 Canada Square
Canary Wharf
London
E14 5AA

Table of Contents

What Is an NDE?

Wikipedia gives the following characteristically unemotional description of an NDE:

A near-death experience (NDE) is a profound personal experience associated with death or impending death which researchers claim share similar characteristics. When positive, such experiences may encompass a variety of sensations including detachment from the body, feelings of levitation, total serenity, security, warmth, the experience of absolute dissolution, and the presence of a light. When negative, such experiences may include sensations of anguish and distress.

If only it was that simple.

I'm one of the 'researchers' who claim they share similar characteristics. Such a short summary to explain one of the most important questions in the history, or indeed the future of humanity.

Interestingly, Wikipedia's description specifically calls out negative experiences of anguish and distress. It should be pointed out that of over 5000 recorded NDE accounts (people who have experienced and reported their experience), I could only find less than 150 Hellish (negative) experiences during the course of my research.

Negative, or Hellish NDE accounts, are estimated to account for between 4% to 15% of all reported NDE's.

The early pages of this book are true to its title. But you cannot explain the negative without the positive. Right now, that won't make any sense to you, but it will. These negative experiences that we will review together are disturbing, terrifying, and horrific. My goal is not to scare you, not for sensationalism or my own personal self-gratification. I take no pleasure in reading these accounts over and over during the course of my research. But it has been my own self-imposed mission to understand the phenomenon of Hell, Demons, and all that this entails.

If you've read other NDE related books, you may ask, "What's different about this one?" This is not a personal account of the author; this is the collective account of hundreds of people from all corners of the Earth that have had an NDE. A single NDE account is incredible and inspiring in its own right, but it doesn't give us the bigger picture. The underlying message is the same, and it's incredibly simple, but you'll have to get to the end of our journey to understand that message, just telling you is not enough.

As I've already mentioned, the overwhelmingly vast majority of NDE's are positive. As a result, it's difficult for someone who has had a positive NDE to accept the existence of Hell and Demons. There is a very good reason for this, which we'll also cover.

My focus has been entirely on holistic analysis and interpretation. Interpretation is important because everything has meaning. If we just read about these incredible people's experiences and call it a day, we'll go away with the fear that we've become so accustomed to through scripture. That just won't do.

There is some science behind NDE's. The most popular method for determining if someone had one of these extraordinary experiences is called the Greyson Scale. The Greyson Scale asks 16 specific questions regarding someone's experience that are common in NDE's. Some of them you may be aware of, such as, 'Did you feel separated from your body?' Whereas others are likely to be new or even surprising to you.

Experiences associated to NDE's you may have heard of include, "Did scenes from your past come back to you?" "Did you feel separated from your body?" or "Did you have a feeling of peace or pleasantness?" Ones you may be less familiar with, unless you've taken an active interest in the subject, include "Were your thoughts speeded up?" "Did you come to a border or point of no return?" or "Were your senses more vivid than usual?"

Each question has a brief unique answer, for example the question, "Did you see deceased or religious spirits?" includes the answers "No", "I sensed their presence" or "I actually saw them."

Each answer is scored from 0 to 2. When these numbers are added up, it gives us an overall score on how likely the experience was an NDE.

There's a lot to digest in these questions and for anyone new to the field of NDE's, it can be quite overwhelming, or you may just think its complete codswallop. But what if it's not? The estimated number of people that have these experiences might surprise you.

The Greyson Scale asks questions that are specific to positive NDE's. There is no scale that exists for negative, less than positive or Hellish experiences. That being said, there are reoccurring themes in Hellish experiences, which we'll cover in the coming chapters.

Introduction

"There are more things in heaven and Earth, Horatio, than are dreamt of in your philosophy."
  – Shakespeare

As true as it was over 400 years ago when Shakespeare penned it, as it is today. We can translate the word 'philosophy' to 'science' for the purposes of our exploration of the various realms of the afterlife.

Humanity has progressed more in the last 150 years than in all human history. We have made incredible discoveries that have elevated our species and our understanding of the universe, whilst paradoxically introducing new and inventive ways of destroying ourselves.

Breakthrough discoveries such as the Higgs-Boson particle, which probably means more to physicists than your average person, is a testament to our curiosity, and at over $4bn to construct, it demonstrates our willingness to invest extraordinary amounts of money into humanity's biggest scientific questions.

Perhaps an easier to digest discovery is the astonishing volume of exoplanets (other planets) discovered, over 3000 planets discovered floating around in the darkness of space, with scientists predicting over 40 billion habitable planets within our galaxy. It wasn't that long ago that we believed Earth was a unique happy accident.

With the ever-looming threat of extinction from weapons of mass destruction or the unabated abuse of our planet, one of these 40 billion planets might well be humanity's only hope of our continued survival. Certainly, this is what Stephen Hawking and Elon Musk believe.

The subject of the universe leads to one of the most important questions facing humanity, one that has been featured extensively in popular culture and has inspired generations of scientists and conspiracy theorists. Are we alone in the universe?

Just 50 years ago the idea that aliens exist would be dismissed as fanatical nonsense, and now we're searching our solar system for signs of microbial alien life.

There is a second fundamental question, a question that has given rise to great human structures around the world. A question that has been posed as long ago as when the written word was invented, over 5000 years ago. A question that has ultimately led to the formation of every religion on Earth. *What happens when we die?*

In my opinion, humans formed religious beliefs to cope with their mortality, or as a way to impose order in a chaotic world. For most of us, regardless of how practiced we are in our faiths, life almost has no meaning if it simply ends in darkness. The loss of a loved one is more bearable if we believe we are going to see them again in an afterlife, particularly for parents who have lost children.

But how do we know, how do we know that there is anything after death? With over 4200 religions worldwide, each with its own take on death, how do we choose what to believe? Many of them promise eternal damnation if we choose the wrong path, if we worship false gods.

There is also an ever-growing swell of secularism, people who choose not to follow any religion. Initially when I began my journey my target audience was always this section of society. From 2005 to 2015, the percentage of non-religious people in the United States grew to nearly a quarter of the entire population. In Europe, the figures are similar. That's a lot of non-believers. I should point out, my objective is never to preach, it's to relay information and interpretation.

This book is not a scientific journal or white paper.

My target audience is not the scientific or research community. I'm not submitting my theory and conclusions for peer review. I'm not a scientist by trade, I'm a regular person, and its regular people this book has been written for.

But as I read hundreds of witness accounts and started to move in NDE social circles, mainly online, I started to realise the research I'm conducting can actually help people. Not any particular group of people either, religious, non-religious, NDE experiencer or not, we're all human and we all suffer heartbreaking tragedy in our lives. Just when I'm thinking I've had to suffer through intense tragedy and pain in my own life, someone comes along and shows me just how lucky I am.

Brenda (not her real name) lost her life partner to a heroin overdose. She stood by him, through every meeting, every relapse until his final moments. And now she asks, "Does he miss me? Does he know I love him? Does he still love me?"

Or Sarah (not her real name) who attempted suicide and had an experience she couldn't explain. She asks, "I was in darkness and I heard laughter, what does it mean?" Much to my surprise, further comments of support were from other people that had attempted suicide. Are we supposed to tell her that she'll 'burn in hell' for all eternity? Is that going to help her through the most painful time in her life? Or perhaps we tell her there's nothing, just blackness and nothing. Most people that attempt suicide are seeking escape from their world, telling them everything just ends, including your consciousness, risks them attempting suicide again. We could just say 'we don't know' or not say anything at all. But that's not what I've learnt. It's not about faith. I've read hundreds of NDE accounts creating a baseline of concepts and experiential elements to validate experiences that align with each other. I've then categorised these experiences into their respective 'buckets' to create a narrative of human experience.

Through this narrative I've analysed each experience and identified relevance between those experiences ultimately putting forward interpretations and conclusions on 'the mechanics of it all'. Of course, I'm still learning, as we've discussed this is not exactly a light subject, it's a question humankind has grappled with since the moment we could speak.

And so I changed the scope of my research, now I would focus on a larger group of society, specifically I would focus on people suffering the loss of a loved one, people who have lost hope in life, people struggling to understand their own NDE, people questioning their faith, people with strong faith but curious of this phenomenon, people who either believe nothing or have 'some sort of belief' in 'something' after death, and finally, people just interested in the subject. So basically everyone.

Then there is the burden of proof. In the age of science, as men and woman orbit our planet from space, there is an ever-growing need among new generations to be presented with evidence of God and an afterlife.

Studies of the Afterlife

This book is not about proving or disproving anyone's belief, be it religious or spiritual. Like any research-based activity, I have read hundreds of accounts and collated my findings into this book. I ask that you be open minded, not gullible.

Imagine a courtroom if you will. For many criminal trials there is an absence of physical evidence, so we rely on witness testimony. Witnesses are brought before the judge and jury to give their testimony, or more commonly referred to as 'giving evidence'. The jury then deliberates on the witness testimony and gives a verdict.

Over the course of this book, you are the jury, NDE's are the witness testimony and I'm the lawyer trying to make sense of it all for you, the jury. There is no judge for good reason, but we'll come to that later. Using this court room analogy, the only thing that separates NDE reports from actual real-life witness testimony is a bible (ironically) and a courtroom. I believe I can confidently speak on behalf of most experiencers of NDE's when I say they would happily put their hand on a bible and swear what they saw 'is the truth, the whole truth and nothing but the truth'. Whilst you may dismiss this sentiment as, 'any crazy person would', you should keep in mind that NDE's are estimated to have been experienced by over 20 million people in the United States, over 50 million in Europe and over 100 million in China. They can't all be crazy, otherwise we have a much bigger social problem on our hands. Statistical Source IANDS & Wikipedia There are bonified paid for studies and research programs for what happens when we finally leave this life. A study being conducted by Dr Sam Parnia, the lead investigator in a research project coordinated by Southampton University's School of Medicine in England, has been developed to flash numbers, pictures, symbols or words from a screen facing up toward the ceiling, that only someone who was literally floating on the ceiling would see. The idea is that when the said experiencer awakes, they can recall the number they saw thereby proving the out of body experience. This research program is being conducted in both the UK and the US, placed strategically in surgical rooms.

Another interesting study conducted in April 2013 didn't quite turn out the way the researcher expected. Dr Steven Laureys conducted a research program where he measured the brain activity of someone who had an NDE. He compared brain activity of regular everyday memories and dreams with the subjects of NDE experiences. Dr Laureys' opinion is that NDE's are the brains way of coping with traumatic experiences. This is a common explanation of NDE's. What Dr Laureys found astonished him and his team. Source:

edition.cnn.com/2013/04/09/health/belgium-near-death-experiences/index.html

The expectation was that NDE 'memories' would match the same brainwaves of memories from a dream or person's internal thoughts, not the external memories of real events such as having breakfast or socialising with friends. What Dr

Laureys discovered was that NDE memories were actually richer (more real is one way to explain it) than everyday waking memories. Dr Laureys conclusion… needs more research. Imagine that, not only were the memories not scientifically hallucinations, they were richer and more vivid than actual human experiences. We'll come back to this as we comb through our witness testimony in later pages.

Generally speaking, there is not enough research into NDE's. As a self-proclaimed researcher myself, it can sometimes be frustrating that the second most important thing that will ever happen to us in our entire lifetimes after birth, is our death, and we know little to nothing scientifically about it. People like Dr Laureys are pioneers in this field, it doesn't matter what they believe, all that matters is truth, and these are the brave men and woman seeking it.

So here we are again, back in our courtroom, calling our NDE witnesses to hear their testimony and draw our own conclusions. In the absence of physical evidence, our witnesses are the closest thing we have to truth.

God and Religion

Before we get started here, it's important you understand it doesn't matter what you believe at this point. If you don't believe in God, a divine being, the creator, or a heavenly father, that's fine. Over 300 of the ~5000 NDE accounts I continue to study are from atheists or agnostics. Equally, it doesn't matter if you follow any particular religion. The underlying message, which we'll eventually come to, is the same. Just roll with it for now.

Because of my inherited religious denomination, Church of England, I was most familiar with the Bible, but I never read it in its entirety. When reminiscing over my sordid and sinful past, I would often turn to religious doctrine to try and understand if I could find salvation for all the things that I had done. According to many religions, I'd done enough to burn in Hell for all eternity. Despite my dodgy past, I'd never actually hurt anyone, but I understood that the Bible considered many things to be a sin, not just violence and cruelty against your fellow human. This concept of a fearful and judgemental God was one thing I could never accept in the Bible or reconcile with my innate belief in a superior divine being. I knew that God loved us, as was described in the Bible. This led me to question something that I now feel so strongly about, I almost feel as though it's an insult to God to suggest it. The idea that God would harm a single human life was something that I could never believe. For me, it made the entire Bible questionable.

The story that sticks with me the most, and is well known in popular culture, is the story of Moses. The final warning Moses gave to the Pharaoh of Egypt was that if he didn't release the Jews, God will kill (yes, kill) the first born of the Egyptians. We're not just talking men and woman; the Pharaoh's own child was merely but an infant. No doubt there were many small children that would have been killed across Egypt if such a thing ever occurred.

We are all the children of God, his most beloved, it is said in the Bible. Would any parent of sound mind murder their own child? What I have come to understand from my research, because it's literally in 100% of credible Greyson scale validated accounts I've studied, is that God has unconditional love for his children, for us. Would a creator, a divine being of pure unconditional love and acceptance, truly murder his own children? Personally, I don't think so, but I wanted to know for sure.

To be fair, it's not just the Bible that preaches divine retribution. The concept of a God that demands subservience and hands out eternal damnation is common among many religions. The good news is that based on the thousands of NDE accounts, our witness statements, not a single credible witness reports God's judgement or anger toward a single person that ever was, or ever will be. In the summer of 1978 Wesley had a near fatal motorcycle accident that left him paralysed for life. During his experience he reported that God said the following to him during his NDE.

"I was afraid to look at him. He laughed and said, 'You humans all have the same belief that you cannot look upon me. Your beliefs and your bible are not completely correct or complete, but they are the best you have, and you must do the best you can with them."

With over 4200 religions on this Earth, many of them teaching that worshipping false idols (believing in the wrong religion), will result in a one-way trip to eternal damnation and torture in Hell, you can begin to understand why more and more people are turning away from religion. Who wants to decide on faith when you have a 4199 in 4200 chance of burning for all eternity? It's not lost on me that not believing is also a ticket to damnation according to many scriptures.

This is not to say that religion is a bad thing; far from it, religion is routed in the right place. It teaches the core principles of good and bad, the importance of treating others equally and to love thy neighbour. Religion also promotes a relationship with God and a healthy outlook on life. Personally, I've never met a bad Christian. Whilst I was born into this denomination, I've had little involvement with the church, but I have many Christian friends and they are some of the finest people I've ever known.

This combined with my own personal battle with drugs, disease and near brushes with death led me to study and research a very specific area of NDE's, Hellish experiences. I've met a lot of really bad people in my life, people that take pleasure in hurting others, people that thrive on fear and intimidation. I wanted to know what fate awaited them, and what post death destiny awaited me.

And just like a good horror movie, people are intrigued, this is a subject that many people I speak to want to hear more about. Aside from the fascination with the concept of Hell, people also have legitimate questions about the existence and purpose of Hell.

Many of us want there to be a Hell, an eternal prison of punishment for the evillest of those that have walked among us. Particularly those that have lost loved ones through acts of murder, or themselves been victims of cruelty. But if God loves us unconditionally, why would he send anyone to Hell? That's even worse than what the Bible said God did to the Egyptians. And if God didn't send the evil people of this world to Hell, does that mean God loves Hitler as much as he loves me? What about his victims? Where is the justice in forgiving murderers and the evillest people in our world? Is there even a Hell? Is religion right, will I go to Hell for not following the prescribed path? If I do, how the Hell do I get out of Hell? How do I avoid Hell? Is it too late? Have my dead loved ones gone there? Are demons and evil spirits real? Do people who commit suicide go to Hell? Arghhhh! Fear not, we will answer all these questions.

I have not personally been to Hell, unless you count certain parts of my life. I've read hundreds of accounts of witnesses who have, and witnesses who have been imparted with knowledge of Hell. As we've already discussed, of the over 5000 NDE reports only a tiny fraction have reported experiencing a Hellish NDE. In the coming pages we will review from our witnesses these experiences and identify common themes and trends. As the lawyer of this story, I'll summarise my findings and present my case to you, the jury, answering those questions that many people ask themselves.

Like any good story, this one has a beginning, a middle and an end. In the beginning we'll review extracts from Hellish experiences and talk about what our witness's saw, felt and experienced. The middle of our story will answer some of the questions we posed a short while ago, and the end of the story will be a review of my findings and theory on Hell.

However, the story doesn't end there. The best stories have a twist. The existence of Hell is intrinsically linked to the existence of Heaven. I wouldn't be doing this story any justice if I didn't 'connect the dots' for you and introduce you to the ultimate lesson.

Hell and Demons

The vast majority of NDE witness's do not encounter any negative emotions or experiences during their NDE. Each NDE is a personal experience with many elements unique to that individual. That being said, there are common themes that run through almost every single experience. The mechanics of these experiences have reoccurring themes, places, feelings, sounds, interactions and even smells.

It's important you understand the context of what led our following witnesses to the depths of Hell. We'll briefly look at the circumstances surrounding each one of these experiences. I haven't included every statement from our witness's, some are short whilst others are most likely resulting from ICU psychosis (hallucinations in intensive care caused by prolonged unconsciousness) or some other factor. We'll focus on the hundreds of those that align with other related experiences.

The following pages will include witness accounts, but I will not use real names or places to protect the identity of those individuals. We'll start with the accounts of Hell and demons. Our witness's had other experiences that either preceded and/or followed their harrowing journey to the darkness and torment of Hell, but we'll just focus on the

Hellish components right now. We will discuss these other events that occurred in their testimonies, as these other experiences are important to our interpretation, but we'll cover them later when we explore the meaning of all this.

Mikey

Mikey is French and had an epileptic seizure whilst having a shower at home. Mikey's Hellish experience starts with a common place of darkness. Not every witness comes to this place, but more do than do not. For Mikey, this dark place would lead to Hell.

"Suddenly I found myself in an alien completely black space. I had no physical form. I couldn't move, but unlike what happened to me in the bathroom it was like I was trapped unable to move even slightly inside a bubble. It was like being held by an intense and incredibly powerful magnetic field. I was powerless to do anything and so I just stayed there, on my own without a single thing happening for what felt like a few minutes to me."

We will dedicate some time analysing this dark place in detail in later pages, sometimes referred to as the Void or, my favourite new term for this place, the Nexus. Both positive and negative witnesses visit this place, what happens next, however, is exclusive to Hellish experiences.

"I suddenly had this feeling of many beings focused on me. They were not visible, but I had this feeling they were small and agile. I saw lots of small lights moving around me. One thing that stood out was bad intent, really BAD intentions, and nothing else. They were evil beings. They were whispering among themselves, but I couldn't make out a word they were saying, it was like being in a horror movie.

As they became excited, they moved around more and more, similar to the way predators circle their prey. I realised I was the prey. They gathered right in front of me. Suddenly they stopped and become completely focused on me. Then it happened, all these beings quickly became still in their places, there was a sense of panic among them. It was like a military formation of soldiers preparing for the arrival of their commander. This didn't feel good at all."

There's a lot to unpack here. The evil intent, the intentions of malice is common in Hellish NDE's. These beings that reside in this place are always full of hatred, desperate to keep our witnesses in this place of evil, and for them to share their agony and torment. We'll see more examples of this evil intent as we continue. If you think of pure evil, it is the intent to cause harm and distress on others. In Hell, these beings, these demons have only one goal, and that is to inflict fear, hatred and pain on the poor souls that find themselves there. But there is something these demons also know, something that troubles them, something that we'll discuss later.

The presence of a leading demon or commander is also not uncommon as we'll see later. It's somewhat surprising that a place of chaos and torment would have a command structure. Unfortunately for Mikey, his experience does not end here.

"It was total silence now. All these creatures in front of me all together started to chant my name, at first it was quiet and weak and then gradually harder and harder. Miiiiikkkeeey, Miiiiikkkeeey, Miiiiikkkeeey, Miiiiikkkeeey. I felt there was sadism in their voices. I felt so uncomfortable. I then felt another presence, Satan. The voices grew louder and louder, from weak muttering to fever pitch excitement. As I moved forward, the larger presence become more apparent, I felt this larger presence was enormous and that I should avoid it at all costs.

MIIIIIKKKEEEY… MIIIIIKKKEEEEY… I tried to move but I couldn't, I couldn't even scream, to howl my terror but I just couldn't do it. Against my will I was forced forward, I tried to back away BUT NO USE!!! I felt there was a point of no return… MIIIIIKKKEEEY… MIIIIIKKKEEEY, MIIIIIKKKEEEY… It was almost a scream now. No! I don't want this! NO-O-O-O-O-O-O-O! NO-O-O-O-O-O-O-O-O-O-O!"

Mikey then regained consciousness from his seizure. Demons tormenting or intimidating people comes up routinely in Hellish experiences. However, I've only ever heard Satan mentioned twice. Part of the reason people have Hellish experiences explains why Mikey felt the presence of Satan. It could also be that Mikey's observation of a larger commander-like figure may conjure up his preconceptions of Satan.

An incredibly common theme shared by both positive and Hellish experiences is the return to their body, often a traumatic experience, for very different reasons. For Mikey, his return was painful because of the experience he brought back with him. Stress in everyday life can cause physical symptoms, we can only imagine the stress Mikey must have had on his return to his body. As you can see below, such an experience can have horrible long terms effects on our witness's.

"As I wrote those last few times on this day, 23rd November, 2013, my entire body is tense. I'm breathing erratically and my pulse is racing. I'm imperceptibly trembling. I feel a weight on my chest. It took me years before I could talk to anyone about this. I've always wondered why my experience ended so suddenly. It has occurred to me that I might be damned."

If I could talk to Mikey, I would tell him not to worry. He is not damned. But it's still early in our journey to draw those conclusions. The trauma of these experiences is often carried by our witnesses into their everyday lives.

When I said earlier that I wanted to help our witness's make sense of their experience, it's people like Mikey I'm talking about, and all those that follow.

Jim

Our next witness is Jim. Jim was told that he had colon cancer. During his treatment, he was given medication that had a chance of causing a heart attack. Unfortunately for Jim, he did suffer a heart attack. Jim's brother had a positive NDE just weeks before his own experience. As with Mikey we'll skip to the beginning of his Hellish experience. We join Jim's experience at the realisation of death.

"I wondered, oh my God, I'm dead. Is this what death is like, but where is my mother and grandfather? My brother spoke of music, but I don't hear it. There's no light that he spoke of. At this point everything became black, I couldn't see a thing and all my thoughts were played back to me.

The place I was in started to fill with fog. I then could feel myself moving along a completely dark hallway. A voice was calling out my name asking me to follow them, they said I was fine and that this was my home. They told me they were there to guide me to my home. I knew something was not quite right and wanted to go back, but I was told there was no going back as my time on Earth was over. I was told to keep moving and I would see my mum soon. The voices kept on hurrying me, there was an urgency in their voices. I felt something wasn't right and that something bad was about to happen to me. Every time I glanced behind me, wanting to go back, the voices told me to keep up and keep moving."

Jim, like most of our other witnesses, found himself in the Nexus. Jim knows something isn't right. Without getting too ahead of ourselves, if you feel something is wrong, then you're probably right. Witnesses who have positive experiences (which is nearly everyone) have a feeling of peace, calm and love in the Nexus. You may feel confused and anxious, but this is almost always temporary. Normally you would find peace in the comfort and tranquillity that surrounds you in the darkness of the Nexus. Jim is also being led by voices he cannot identify or see where they are coming from. This is not something positive witness's experience, they may hear a voice, but it's not long before they realise whose voice it is, or that the voice means them nothing but love.

Another common experience is what I refer to as 'instantaneous understanding'. We'll come to an extensive section on this, but for now, just know that in almost all cases, except Hellish experiences, the witness understands instantly everything that is communicated to them. In Jim's case, he does not have this understanding. He continues to follow the voices.

"I decided enough was enough and told them I didn't want to follow them any further until they told me where we were and where we were going. The voices told me we had reached our destination, that I was where I was supposed to be.

"Suddenly there was this smell of what I thought was sulphur and death. The voices began to laugh and told me that the actions of my life are why I am here. I again asked where this was and what was going to happen. The voices just laughed even more and keep on repeating what I was saying. Then I thought this must be Hell, this is definitely not what happened to my sister in her experience, this is not how she described Heaven. Even though I was thinking this, I could hear my thoughts out loud. The voices responded to this and told me there was no Heaven for me, that this place was my Heaven. One of the voices than said that it was feeding time."

Jim has been deceived. Another common trait of evil, to lie and deceive. Not only are these demons deceiving Jim in the obvious sense, by telling him that he'll see his mother again, but they are also deceiving him in other ways. Jim is not here because of his life choices, and he certainly isn't being prevented from entering Heaven.

One thing the Demons said that is accurate, which will make more sense when we draw our conclusions, is when they told Jim that this was 'his heaven'.

We haven't touched on one of the more disturbing aspects of Hell, torture. This is where the contrast of Hellish and positive experiences become so clear. For positive, or Heavenly experiences, a person no longer has a physical body to be tortured. This is an important distinction, as it tells us something about what point Jim is at on his journey through the afterlife. Like many pieces of the puzzle we're figuring out, retaining a physical form is a clue to solving this puzzle of Hell. But Jim knows nothing of the mechanics of his experience, and so it continues.

"Suddenly I was thrown backwards against a wall with my arms pinned against the wall. There was nothing I could do, I was helpless. Then I saw what looked like hair ball creatures with sharp rows of teeth come at me. I could now see that these creatures were transforming from little hair balls back to monsters over and over. They were the most disgusting ugly looking things I've ever seen and have ever seen since. They had the appearance of snakes mixed with bats with something that had horns. Their bodies were snake-like with wings. Their arms and hands were like bats. Their faces looked like snakes with fangs like a bat and a snake. On their heads they had horns that didn't resemble anything from Earth, they were pointed and shaped in an unearthly way.

"Whilst they transformed into their hairball shape, I asked them what was happening to me. They just laughed at me telling me to shut up. Every feeling I had inside my head came out loud so they could hear it. They started to come at me, I felt sick to my stomach. I recall thinking why is this happening to me? Where is my family and where is God? They started to feed on me. I looked down and saw that my body parts were missing, as I looked up, I could see my body parts in their mouths.

One of them then said, 'We told you already that this is your heaven, and we are your God.'"

This is clearly a disturbing and terrifying experience. Being eaten alive does occur often in other Hellish experiences. If you imagine the most terrifying thing that could happen to us, being eaten alive whilst having to remain conscious through the experience must be in the top five.

Jim also describes the demons that are torturing him. Whilst there are common themes, unlike positive experiences, the physical characteristics of demons change whilst maintaining some common themes. Seeing creatures with various Earthly animal like characteristics is common, such as snakes, spiders, and bats. What is unique about Jim's Demons is the 'hairballs' with teeth. At this point take note of the fact that the Demons Jim is being tortured by resemble similar features described by theological scripture.

Slavic scripture describes a demon called Bukavac, a six-legged monster with gnarled horns. In Hebrew scripture Belial is a demon with wings and horns. Balam is a Christian demon with three heads, a Ram, a man and a Bull, riding a Bear. As with other features of our witness's Hellish experiences, there is a reason why these demons resemble creatures of myth, theological scripture and legend.

Jim's experience did not end where we left off, but it did go in an entirely altogether different direction. Why and how Jim's experience changed is part of the answer to one of our key questions regarding Hell, and as such has the appropriate analysis and interpretation in our later sections. In that section we'll revisit Jim's experience and finish his story.

Alexandra

Alexandra is a mother with a drinking addiction. Many of our witness accounts include people with addiction problems. Whether it's drugs or alcohol, the disease of addiction commonly ends up as the cause of suicide attempts among our witnesses. In 1994 Alexandra attempted suicide. It's important to note that anyone that feels suicide is the only solution to their problem, already has feelings of guilt, a lack of self-worth and hopelessness. Whilst this may be obvious, it's important to remember this as we head towards our conclusion on the purpose, or existence of Hell. We start with Alexandra's arrival at the hospital after her son found her turning blue.

"When we got to the hospital, I started to descend into darkness. My body remained in the hospital, but I found myself falling down a pitch-black tunnel.

"Demons were suddenly all around me, and although I didn't have a physical body, they were feverishly ripping my flesh off. It was so incredibly painful. As I was dragged further and further into Hell, I saw lots of historical figures, and then I saw my father. He turned to me and welcomed me to Hell.

At this point I was convinced this was it for me. My life on Earth was done, and I've ended up in Hell.

"Getting out of Hell would be impossible."

Alexandra found herself in a similar situation to Jim. Her flesh being torn away by demons. Her responses to specific NDE questions included horrific screams and evil laughter, which is also common in Hellish experiences. Note that she is already resigned to her fate, she believes she belongs in Hell forever and will never escape.

Interestingly, Alexandra saw her father; she didn't talk about her father beyond seeing him in her testimony, but I suspect she had a bad relationship with him and thus views him as cruel, unkind, or evil. Alexandra returns to her body, but instead of becoming conscious in her physical body, she returns to an out of body experience.

"Suddenly, I was moving away from the demons and started to go back up the tunnel towards my body. I did not go back completely. I remained separate from my body, observing the doctors work on it. They were attempting to stabilise my vital signs and flush all the drugs and alcohol out of my system so the toxins would not continue to ravish my body. I was shocked at what they were doing to my body but was relieved the demons were not tearing my flesh off anymore. Eventually, after what felt like an eternity, my heart started to beat in a relatively normal fashion, and I started breathing through a ventilator. I was pulled towards, and then into my body."

Alexandra's testimony is short. Prior to Alexandra's experience she was an atheist and now she practices New Age spirituality. The vast majority of people who experience positive or negative NDE's return to Earth with new or reinforced faith. Many witnesses start or switch to practicing spiritual belief systems as opposed to traditional religion. Atheists are no different.

If you're strongly religious and believe that non-believers belong in Hell, then this would explain Alexandra's experience. Equally, if you believe that people who commit suicide belong in Hell, then this experience checks all the boxes. The belief that people who commit suicide go to Hell is a common belief among even 'the slightly religious'. It was something I believed prior to my journey. But neither of these explanations explain why Alexandra is in Hell. Our previous witnesses were of sound mind and had led normal kind lives, so why were they in Hell? Among witnesses of NDE's, this is a common question, "Why do good people have Hellish NDE's?" The answer is the same for all of us, regardless of how kind or cruel we are.

Katheryn

Katheryn, like Alexandra, has a short testimony. Unlike Alexandra she didn't attempt suicide, but instead took one of her friends' sleeping tablets to help her sleep. She misjudged the dosage and took too many. Her boyfriend found her unconscious and not breathing on the kitchen floor, the sleeping tablets left her unconscious for four days.

"I remember it was completely black. I couldn't see a thing, but I could hear horrific screaming and sounds of angry animals or demons. They were terrible sounds. The smell was indescribable. If I had to describe it, I would say it smelt rancid at best. I just couldn't move. I felt claws and teeth clawing at my skin. I was being torn apart into pieces and eaten. The pain was unimaginable, like nothing I've felt before. I didn't die. I couldn't make a sound or scream, and I couldn't get away. It didn't make sense how I was being torn apart over and over. My limbs had been ripped off many times and there was something eating my stomach, but I didn't lose consciousness or die. The suffering just continued. I eventually realised I was in Hell and I was dead. This was going to be my eternity. At this point I started to wake up."

The starting point for most Hellish experiences is the Nexus. This is not always the case for positive NDE's, where many people find themselves in a tunnel or immediately in the company of loved ones.

Whilst Kathryn's testimony is short, it's descriptive. Kathryn refers to the 'smell' of Hell. When I read my first account that included a smell, I was surprised. According to a 1998 study, the percentage of 3,372 regular dreams that had a scent or smell was only 0.1%. In contrast, out of over 150 reports, Hellish experiences mention the smell of Hell at around 25%. This number would likely be higher if the question was specifically asked as part of the testimony, however, we only have this information when it's volunteered.

When asked to elaborate on voices and sounds, Kathryn gives more detail on what she heard and saw.

"I heard a voice I could not identify. There were screams far off in the distance that echoed everywhere. I couldn't hear any speaking, just screams of suffering and pain. I heard the sound of my body being repeatably torn apart and the sound of my bones snapping. I could hear the sound of something eating my stomach, it was horrific.

"Although my arms and legs had been bitten off and eaten, they were being torn off and eaten again and again."

Sam

A shorter account by Sam in 2007 describes a similar situation after he contracted a flesh-eating bacteria which led to cardiac arrest.

"At that moment, I was suspended in darkness, naked and cold. I could feel the presence of evil all around me. I kept trying to speak, but my mouth was sealed shut, as my body was frozen, no movement. I saw my wife reaching out to me, but she was going in the warm and comfortable direction."

Sam is in a cold darkness, this time, however, our witness is naked. This is also a common theme, a form of humiliation. In other instances, humiliation may take the form of taunts or mocking as it relates to a person's relationships, or the life they have led. Physical sensations are relatively unique to Hellish experiences. In retrospect positive experiences describe a complete detachment from physical sensation, particularly pain. In many cases a positive witness leaves their body during their moment of death therefore sparing them the pain they would have otherwise experienced. It's almost like they are being saved from the impending agony of death. This will be a comfort to many of us that fear the sensation or suffering of death.

Francesca

A young woman, Francesca, took a drug overdose in 1973. Not an intentional overdose, she was taking Acid (LSD, a hallucinogenic) with friends, took some downers (drugs that bring you down from a high, such as Valium or Xanax). Against her will her friends injected her with another drug, she fought back but was already too wasted to fight them off. In her desperation she took a bite at one of her friends. Francesca was carried to her car by her friends, they then proceeded to the hospital. Due to Francesca's spiralling state of mind she jumped out of the car. Her friends gave up and left her to her own fate on the side of the road, clearly not friends after all. Eventually the police arrived and arrested her. In typical fashion for someone as high as Francesca was, she attempted to fight back, she was hog-tied and taken to the police station. It wasn't long before the police realised taking her to the station was a bad idea. She had trouble breathing and ultimately ended up at the hospital. Francesca's descent into darkness starts here.

"I was hovering above the hospital bed, watching them trying to revive me. All of a sudden I was surrounded by monstrous creatures, I called them 'dark angels'. They were

chanting at me, 'Out of the light and into the darkness…' I don't remember the rest of the chant. They were tearing at me and it was incredibly painful, taking pieces out of me until I was nothing. This all happened whilst flying down the hallways of the hospital and through the roof."

This is our first witness that experiences torture during an out of body experience. Out of body experiences are common, as are meetings with beings during this process. The key difference is that in the majority of cases these beings are beings of light and are there to guide the witness to Heaven. When an addict, whether it's alcohol or drugs, leaves their body, they are no longer under the influence of drugs or alcohol, but in the case of hellish experiences, any confusion, fear or anger they were feeling at the time goes with them. These demons also chant *'Out of the light and into the darkness'*. For positive NDE's, darkness is not symbolic of evil, pain or suffering. As we've discussed previously. Positive witnesses typically describe the darkness as peaceful, tranquil, and filled with overwhelming feelings of love.

Francesca's experience continues.

"The next thing that happened was that I found myself in Hell. I was flat on my back with metal bars pressing down on me. I was surrounded by the sound of souls crying in anguish. An evil presence asked me questions for what seemed like forever. It asked me what I believed and who I worshipped. It asked me about my spirituality. I was terrified at first but became defiant as it continued to question me and challenged it's right to keep me there. I told this evil being I believed in

Jesus and that I didn't think it could hurt me. Suddenly I was no longer in Hell."

Francesca was returned to her body immediately after leaving Hell.. The Demons tormenting Francesca are interested in her faith. They didn't specifically mention a denomination, such as Christianity, but they wanted to know who she worshipped. At the time Francesca was Christian, and yet she was not questioned about any particular religious figures. After her experience, she converted to Buddhism, a spiritual faith that focuses heavily on the concept that existence is a never-ending process of reincarnation.

'Take note of the fact that Francesca consciously decided she did not belong in Hell. There are various reasons we could draw from her statement as to the reason she was able to depart from Hell. Was she saved by Jesus? Was it her return to life that saved her? Or was it something else?

Mandy

Mandy struggled with Anorexia on and off her entire life. Unfortunately, Mandy started to lose her battle with Anorexia in 2014. After separating from her husband due to an affair, Mandy's condition further deteriorated. One day her husband came to reconcile and so they decided to take a walk on a nearby beach to talk. Mandy describes what happened next.

"My husband noticed I suddenly changed and asked, 'What's wrong?' The only words I could come out with were, 'Blood, sugar,' to which he responded, 'Where are your tablets?' With what little energy I had, I responded, 'Bag, home.' Instinctively we both quickly stood up and made our way across the beach. I figured I had a minute or two before I crashed and thought I would make it to the car.

"I only made it two steps when I suddenly left my body. My husband later told me I just oozed to the ground. It felt like my body just couldn't contain me anymore and that it was just too heavy for me. As I was leaving my body, I managed to get out my last sentence saying, 'I thought I had more time, I didn't make it to Disney World.' My husband pleaded with me to get up, but I couldn't resist the urge just to lie there. I wanted to tell him I was comfortable where I was, it was so

peaceful. He would have let me stay there if he knew how it felt. I could feel the sensation of him holding his fingers against my neck trying to get a pulse. I felt some guilt for not trying harder to sit upright, but I was determined to leave.

"As I looked down at my body on the beach, I was thinking what a beautiful blessing this is! I died at my favourite place on the whole planet! Now I was in space surrounded by a golden colour, I could feel it as well as see it. It was warm and comforting. Images started to roll in front of my eyes like a movie reel. With each scene I saw pure love, I perceived it through the eyes of God, not my own. Everything that ever happened to me made sense, all of the abuse, the rejection, hate, anger and abandonment. Everything that had happened meant something. God wept with me at one point, I felt more love than humanly possible. I had become love.

"There was no reason for me to go back to the world.

"I was done with that now. I had a split second to tell my husband something. I attempted to say, 'I love you so much,' but what I actually said was 'I LOVED you so much. Tell my boys I love them and always will.' I sensed a hand on my chest and my last breath left me. I saw my heart stop and my eyes closing. Now there was nothing, just an empty void."

Mandy had clearly decided she was no longer for this world, and so far, her experience seems to be consistent with a positive transition to the afterlife. Feelings of love, joy and understanding are all trademarks of positive experiences. Experiences that start positive and descend into Hellish experiences are rare. The feelings Mandy describes are consistent with other positive experiences, an overwhelming sense of love and even seeing through the eyes of God. But things are about to take a sinister turn for Mandy.

"Bad things started happening. I could feel something being ripped from me. I can only describe it as a demon. I groaned out loud as it was happening. My husband said that it sounded like something was coming out of the pits of Hell. I started flying forwards toward something that seemed like a barrier. Evil spirits were chasing me that looked mostly like snake-like figures. A voice asked me, 'Mandy, what do you know to be true of Jesus Christ?' I answered, 'That he died on a cross for me.'"

What makes Mandy's experience unique is that her husband witnessed a part of her experience. Whilst rare, it has happened more than once. Mandy also witnesses animal-like demons with strikingly similar characteristics to our other witnesses'. The moment of death is no doubt a traumatic experience, even when we're saved from the physical pain of it. We can only imagine what must be going through the mind of a person that knows they are about to die. We can accurately surmise that most people look back at the life they've led, and as a result any trauma will likely be a part of that conscious process. Mandy's story doesn't end there, but as with our other witnesses', we'll come back to Mandy's story soon.

Olivia

In the early '70s after lifesaving bladder surgery, Olivia became addicted to opioids. Olivia was suddenly taken off her opioid pain medication without consideration for the serious withdrawal that would follow. A combination of serious withdrawal, an unhappy marriage and post-surgery depression led Olivia to a drug overdose, and she ultimately attempted suicide. As with our other witness's Olivia's story starts in blackness.

"It was complete blackness, it was empty, I didn't feel anything at all. My dad told me that there is nothing when you die, just nothing at all. I remember thinking that if this was true, how would I even perceive this nothingness? I could feel that I was surrounded by emptiness and that I was a part of this emptiness, I felt I was empty as well. I started to hear voices that started quietly but quickly got louder and louder until it was a deafening sound.

"The sounds of voices were soon joined by the sound of chaos. It was approaching me from below. Suddenly something started grabbing at my legs, calves and ankles like it was desperately trying to pull me down somewhere. I wasn't on anything solid at this point, I was floating while something

frantically was trying to pull me down. I could feel that whatever it was, it was hopeless, angry, and tortured. There were many of them and they all desperately wanted me to be as tortured and hopeless as they were."

We've seen this before, the desire by these beings to pull other souls into their torment and pain. Olivia doesn't describe demons, but the behaviour of these beings is in keeping with the behaviours we've observed by demons in previous witness accounts. Regardless of the form of these beings, they are desperately attempting to pull Olivia into their midst.

"I was frozen scared, I remember it well. It was so confusing, I didn't know what was happening. The lower down I was pulled, the colder it became. As I was pulled to the place of these beings, it felt squishy and wet, and it continued to get colder. Now the beings were ripping and tearing at me. I wanted to leave, I wanted to go home."

Olivia woke up to her husband shaking her shortly after wishing to return home. Something we haven't seen before is a description of the environment. Olivia describes a squishy and wet environment, this has been described by other Hellish witnesses. Is it a coincidence that Olivia returned to life after wishing to go home, or was there something else at play here?

Mel

Our next witness's interview came with a warning from Dr Jeffrey Long, the author of the bestselling title we've already discussed, *The Light Beyond*. Dr Long starts the commentary with, "This hellish NDE is so graphic and atypical; I think an attached commentary is appropriate." Before we get into the witness account, it's important we review the context.

In 2002, Mel was with her friend, Gary, they were arguing about something in Mel's words, 'stupid'. Gary was driving his father's car, both he and Mel had been drinking and Gary was not supposed to be using his father's car. According to Mel, Gary was not a nice person, he was mean and aggressive. In the heat of the argument Gary floored the accelerator pedal and did a sharp turn to scare Mel. The next thing Mel remembers is being wheeled into a large room at the hospital.

"What happened next is incredibly vivid. I remember it well. I quickly started to float out of my body and got sucked through a tunnel of light, like I was on a hallucinogenic drug or something. I didn't know where I was headed but I couldn't control it anyway. I couldn't run or anything. At first, I thought I was heading to heaven, but something happened,

and I suddenly stopped dead. Like a bolt of lightning, I started to fall faster and faster and faster.

I felt I'd fallen straight down toward a black hole of sorts. It was dark but I felt I could cut through it with a knife. As I was falling, I began to hear screams, cries of people suffering horrific pain and the most disturbing horrible laughing. The smell was the most putrid smell imaginable. The blackness started to fill with fire as if I was falling into a massive furnace. When the fire reached me, it consumed me, I started to scream but I couldn't hear my own screams, I didn't know where they were going but I was screaming at the top of my voice.

"I hit something hard when I landed on my back, it felt like rocks. I felt terrible pain over whatever this new form was."

The sensation of falling is not uncommon in Hellish NDE's. Mel's description of a putrid smell is consistent with other descriptions we've seen so far. The horrible screams, the audible agonising pain and the fire is also consistent with what we've already encountered. But it gets much worse than any other account we've seen so far, and certainly any account I've ever read.

"When I opened my eyes, I realised I was not on my own. There were these distorted creatures grasping at me, they began to drag me towards gigantic black gates. As I kicked and screamed, I was yelling at the top of my voice for Allah, Buddha or God, whoever I could remember learning about in Religious Education classes, but nothing came. I recall a giant creature started ripping at the skin on my back with

what felt like sharp nails whilst another began to rip my hair so hard I wanted to throw up.

"Another creature kicked me over and stood on my chest laughing, saying things to me about personal issues he somehow knew all about. Things like my mum dying when I was born, my sister going into prison and about Gary driving the car that killed me. The thing that sticks so hard in my mind is the smell, vile like rotting flesh and burnt hair. The sinister laughs and taunts at me could barely be heard over the roaring sounds of fire all around me.

"I then saw people running and screaming all around me. Some children not much older than twelve years old were crying whilst being harassed and pulled apart by these horrible malevolent creatures.

"I remember well seeing Gary (the guy driving the car), he was hanging upside down on a cross with nails hammered into his feet and hands, like Jesus on the cross. The creatures were all whipping him at the same time chanting in a foreign language I've never heard before.

"The cross he was nailed to was now on fire and had spread to his hands, chest and head melting and peeling his skin off, he was absolutely TERRIFIED!!! He was begging them to stop as he cried in agony."

There is a lot to go through here, the description of Mel's torment is explicit, she provides a lot of detail. Her experience includes taunts, physical torture, an unknown language and disturbingly she includes children in her account. Positive witnesses have described passing over with companions who shared their fate, but this is the only account I've read where a companion joins our witness in Hell. Take note of the symbolic nature of Mel's account, an upside-down cross, Gary nailed to the cross and the fires burning across the landscape. Mel's experience ends in the hospital.

"My body or spirit, or whatever you want to call it, started to suddenly seriously burn from all the fire on the ground. I started crying out for God again saying, 'God, please help me.' As I did this, the creatures got angry and became frustrated, hurting me even more. 'God, please,' I finally begged. Just as I was about to give up a great suction pulled me from their grasp and took me up back through the tunnel. I then awoke to the sounds of a woman's voice, the doctor.

"A couple of hours later when I'd recovered a little, the doctors told me that Gary didn't make it. They said his heart gave up during resuscitation, it just gave up the fight. He died 30 minutes before I woke up."

Unfortunately, Gary did not make it, but Mel survived. The most important thing to take from Mel's experience is when she said, "*'God, please,' I finally begged seconds before deciding to give up.*" 'Giving up' are the wrong words to describe what Mel did, in actual fact Mel 'let go'.

Not surprisingly, Mel became a devout Christian after her experience. In the absence of any other explanation she sought out religion.

Purgatory

So far, we've focused entirely on the traditional experiences of Hell and demons. But there is another level of Hell, one that commonly comes up among those who attempt suicide. A place of hopelessness, loneliness, and madness. I call this place Purgatory, as it's the closest phrase to describing the nature of this place. In Christianity and Catholicism, Purgatory is a temporary punishment where souls go to be purified before moving onto Heaven. For the purposes of our journey, Purgatory is a place where the hopeless and confused go. If you've ever suffered any form of mental illness, whether it's a side effect of medicine or something more permanent, mental health decline can be just as frightening, if not more frightening than physical illness.

Rachel

We start with Rachel, in 1998 she was at a party taking drugs and inhaling Nitrous. Inhaling any kind of chemical is bad news for our lungs. Gaseous chemicals can quickly clog up our airways, as was the case for Rachel, when she decided to inhale Nitrous directly from a Nitrous tank, instead of the balloons she was using up until this point.

"I was suddenly in a very dark place, the last thing I remember before that was the tank. I instantly understood that I had 'killed myself' and I felt horrible about it. I didn't appear to have any form, only my thoughts. What I considered to be my body felt like balls repelling each other. I felt like I hated myself so much that I was about to explode. This feeling felt like I was on fire, but not because I actually was on fire, it was just because I felt like I was coming apart. I could only think about how I hated myself in this completely lonely place. I came to the realisation that this place would be my eternal punishment."

Rachel immediately decided that she killed herself, this is her state of mind going into her experience. She hated herself for what she had done. Rachel's experience did not end there, we'll come back to her experience during our interpretation.

There is a reason I consistently come back to a witness's state of mind when they have their experience. I'm not just referring to the witness's state of mind, or their emotional state at that exact moment in time, it's their long-term emotional state that is important.

Anastasia

Anastasia has endured terrible pain and suffering in her life. Abused as a child, forced into child pornography and prostitution she soon became addicted to drugs and alcohol. In the late '90s, as a young adult, Anastasia's physical condition worsened, suffering from insomnia her body eventually gave up on her. Anastasia's experience started with a positive experience.

"I was in a hospital room. All of a sudden, this bright golden white surrounded me. It shone off into the distance, I was seeing this light as though it were superimposed over the landscape through the window. Then, I was pulled towards this light. It was the most incredible feeling of peace and love, impossible to put into words, never had I experienced such a feeling before. It was absolute ecstasy. My soul was alive! The feeling was like streams of cool, endlessly flowing water running through it and it was the most invigorating feeling! I didn't want it to stop and I was truly happy for the first time in my life! I was ecstatic in this state of bliss for what seemed like time did not exist. I was aware of everything, I knew everything and I understood everything; nothing was

unknown. I felt unconditional love, all of the questions I had were being answered.

"I stayed like this for a while and then all of a sudden my negative past consumed me. I hadn't dealt with the trauma and pain of my past, I was overwhelmed by it. All the guilt, pain and suppressed anger flowed back into my heart, but it was amplified and saturated me. I felt as though I did not deserve what I just experienced, I didn't deserve all that peace, all I had in my mind were nasty negative thoughts about myself. I reverted to my life long natural state of crippling depression.

"This was the most horrible thing anyone could imagine. I experienced complete blackness. There was no light, there was nothing."

Coming back to our discussion of the mental and emotional states of our witnesses, Anastasia's account was a light bulb moment for me. Her experience further validated my interpretation, which we'll come to soon. Her experience started positive, but then descended into an uncomfortable darkness. What could have caused this?

What changed that took Anastasia from a place of overwhelming love to a place of darkness? There are many aspects of her positive experience that may seem fantastical to you after reviewing our witness's Hellish NDE's. But rest assured, Anastasia's positive experience accounts for nearly all NDE's. As with our Hellish witnesses, we'll also touch on positive witness experiences. Anastasia's experience continues.

"All of a sudden there were these beings surrounding me. I don't know the number, but I felt that they had been in my presence for a while. They had been waiting for me. They started grabbing at me and dragged me to a place of absolute desperation. There was nothing but this horrific void. The void was a complete absence of God. It was absolute torture and desperation, nothing can describe the pain. My deepest nightmare had come true. I was told that my entire family was damned to be in the void and that it was because of me, my actions. Even speaking about this is incredibly difficult. It was pure terror and despair."

Whilst Anastasia's account does include what we can only assume are demons, they do not physically torture her. They know her greatest fear is hopelessness and therefore lead her to Purgatory. Anastasia has suffered deep depression through her life and so she carried it with her when she passed over, except these feelings of anger and a lack of self-worth were amplified.

"I returned back to my body in the hospital. When I tried to tell people what happened to me, they just thought I was crazy. My fiancé left me shortly after I told him what had happened to me. I recovered from my injuries but never recovered emotionally. My experience destroyed my faith in anything. I was terrified that I would eventually spend all of eternity in that blackness. There were many people there."

Unfortunately for Anastasia, the people closest to her did not believe her. This is incredibly common among people who have had an NDE. In many cases the first time they talk about their experience is years later, sometimes decades. Adjusting to an NDE is not just a challenge for our witnesses, loved ones also struggle with the person 'that returns'. Surprisingly, this is a problem for positive experiences as well as negative. Witnesses that harboured bitterness and were generally unkind prior to their positive experience came back as thoughtful and considerate individuals. This can be difficult for loved ones that have become accustomed to their previous behaviours to adjust to.

Cindy

In 1972 Cindy was the victim of an attempted murder. She was poisoned and quickly descended into darkness. Prior to Cindy's experience she held no religious beliefs, in her own words she only had 'contempt for God'.

"The poisoning affected me badly, I suddenly couldn't hear, I couldn't move any of my limbs and I soon fell into a blackness. All of a sudden, I was falling as if I was in an elevator dropping from the top of a skyscraper. It was completely dark with no sound at all, you could hear a pin drop. When I stopped falling, I was deep inside a place devoid of light or anything else. I soon realised I was no longer alive. I knew that I was alone, I knew God wasn't with me.

"The quiet was soon filled by the most awful wailing and distressed cries. I didn't know what it was in the beginning, but I soon realised it was the sound of countless souls in grief and anguish, it was unbearable to listen to.

"They didn't talk, or speak, they were just weeping and wailing. It was the most pitiful and tormented sound I'd ever experienced in my life. In this darkness there was only the sound of the anguish and emptiness. I wanted to leave, but I had no physical form and I couldn't talk. Eventually I found

my voice, deep in my soul I screamed out as loud as I could, I
heard my voice echoing through the darkness over and over.
I heard my screams. 'God, help me!'"

Cindy's experience is in line with other witnesses' who've reported Purgatory. The grief, the cries and the wailing are all consistent with other reports. It's easy to confuse this place with the more traditional Hell we covered in our previous pages, but there are some key differences. Complete darkness, no beings to communicate with, and the silence is distinctly different from traditional Hellish experiences where we've heard about roaring fires, agonising screams, and horrific laughing.

We've now covered the two realms of Hell. You may have heard of other realms, especially if you're religious or have read NDE's from religious figures. When reading any account of death or the afterlife, it can be easy to get lost in other's belief systems and opinions. This is precisely why we review many witness accounts and not just one, it makes our information more reliable and credible. That is not to discount a singular NDE, but to compare it with what other witnesses have experienced so we can discount reports that may serve a person's own personal agenda, as opposed to serving the truth. The number of reports I've come across that are clearly advancing an individual's agenda, such as reinforcing theological or religious ideals, appear routinely. The majority of embellished or misleading accounts I've read, are clearly a reflection of the persons beliefs, or religious denomination. I've come across this with Pastors and Priests many times. You might hear that there is a Hell for each type of sin you've committed, or an angry and judgemental God that is disappointed in you and condemns you to one of these levels of Hell. I've not once come across this from any witness that isn't a religious figure.

There's nothing wrong with preaching your beliefs but using NDE's as a vehicle for preaching fear and judgement is straight up dishonest. It diminishes the testimony of the many witnesses who have come back renewed and full of hope and are keen to share their message.

It may seem ironic that I'm standing up against judgement and condemnation when we've spent the entire first part of this book talking about Hell, but as you'll come to learn why Hell exists and why people end up there, you'll understand why it's so important not to spread messages of fear, judgement and condemnation.

Communication and Knowledge in the Afterlife

The subject of the afterlife is incredibly complex, which is to be expected. There have been many moments in human history where people have looked upon things of great wonder without the slightest idea of how to explain them. Crossing over into another realm is the pinnacle of human wonder. People who go there are faced with realities that surpass the imagination of even the most ambitious storytellers. Throughout human history we have feared that which we do not understand, fear turns to hatred and hatred turns to violence. Something that has been lacking in the accounts of Hell we've already discussed is 'understanding'.

Our witnesses thus far have been confused and afraid. This is not what the vast majority of NDE witnesses experience, there are some similarities, specifically the mode of communication. However, for positive NDE's it goes far beyond communication, it includes instant understanding of both what is communicated and what is felt.

Psalm 19:3 They Speak Without a Sound or Word

Consistent among both Hellish and positive accounts, regardless of how the experience unfolds, be it in Heaven, Hell or out of body on Earth, is the mode of communication. There are no human words in this realm, there are no languages. You cannot think one thing and say another. You cannot hide what you are thinking. This is one of the most profound differences to our physical forms and one of the harder concepts to describe.

Many people use the term telepathic, but telepathic communication is still a linear form of communication and does not describe the method of dialogue in the realm of the afterlife appropriately. Telepathy ultimately is a series of words and sentences that form understanding that are communicated via brainwaves. Here are a series of extracts from separate experiences.

"'Where am I?' The Light answered me, not in words but in thought-concepts." Cristael – 1998

"Although I was aware of my accident, I had no speech. It was more of a thought transfer or telepathy." – Scott, 2014

"It was like telepathy, but more direct." – Caren, 1993

An accurate description from one witness was to call it an 'impression'. This is an apt term to use. When souls communicate, there is instantaneous understanding, there is no doubt, no ambiguity, and no hiding your thoughts. As a soul receives communication, if that communication includes an experience, more than just an acknowledgement for example, the recipient lives that experience within that moment. When knowledge is imparted, it is instantly understood, the meaning, the context, the emotions, and all the experiences related to that knowledge are all instantly known by the recipient.

The soul's ability to process information can be compared to a computer analogy. Take for example the first computers. Let's say a computer from the 1990s would take weeks to calculate a complex mathematical problem. In 2010 a computer could process this same problem in minutes. By the time quantum computers arrive, the same calculation would be almost instant. The soul is immeasurably more advanced than the human brain, it's more comparable to a quantum computer and therefore can process complex experiences coupled with emotions and context instantly. An entire lifetime can be communicated and experienced in the blink of an eye.

"I had complete understanding, collective but separate. Everything made sense. Everything was more vivid, the colours were brighter and deeper." – Kristy, 2000

"With the level of understanding I had at the time, I saw that he took on an image so that I could relate and feel comfortable." – Teri, 1973

"There is total understanding without even experiencing the thought of needing to understand. It is already there – total understanding in perfect clarity." – Bobbi, 1976

"Jesus laughed and then gave me the answer, not in words but in a 'knowing'." – Terry, 1970

"They answered almost at the same instant that I asked them." – Judy, 1967

In Hellish experiences emotions and feelings are also communicated. Witnesses instantly know that these souls wish them harm and torment, they want the experiencer to feel what they feel. Where beings such as demons have been reported, communication is also instant. However, I have yet to read a report of 'impressions' being made in Hellish environments. There is an absence of understanding. This could be because beings bent on malice and torment are able to conceal their true intentions or thoughts. If a tormented being or soul was unable to conceal their true intent, deceit would not be possible.

Beings in this realm seek to confuse and terrify people.

Proverbs 2:1 Turning Your Ear to Wisdom and Applying Your Heart to Understanding

Understanding, or knowledge, is not only imparted through direct communication. Thousands of accounts include instant understanding of the entire universe, in some cases how things work at a molecular level.

"Instantly, my head was flooded with knowledge. As I stared at the boulder, I knew its chemical composition, could describe every curve concavity and convex structure with mathematical formula that were both known to me and yet unknown. I couldn't believe how clear my thoughts were." – Michael, 1966

"Such understanding of life, God, all that is. I remember it was as if I was being re-introduced – or awakening after a hard sleep. I thought questions and they were immediately answered." – Michelle, 1991

"There came sensations of boundless love and boundless understanding. I was everywhere and everything in the universe, yet I was somewhere in particular." – Roger, 1978

"The clarity and understanding I obtained in this state is almost indescribable. Words seem to limit the experience." – Anita, 2006

In many cases this understanding starts from the moment of death, whereas in other cases understanding and knowledge comes later during the experience.

Imagine being able to ask any question about any subject and get a full and truthful answer. You could ponder personal questions about your life and relationships, or more profound questions such as the origins of life and the universe.

Hell Is What You Make It

I mentioned at the beginning of this book that this story has a beginning, a middle and an end. Before we fully launch into the middle of our journey, which contains interpretation and explanation, there are some things you need to understand. Our journey so far has been dark, frightening, and horrific, much like so many lives on Earth. But that's not how most Hellish experiences end.

Some religions teach that Hell is eternal damnation. For most of our witnesses, they were in Hell for a matter of minutes. In some cases, they returned to their body, in other cases they went somewhere entirely different. That's not to say people don't end up there for a long time, we just don't have enough information or witness testimony to make that statement.

Throughout the preceding pages I've frequently referred to the emotional state of our witnesses. It's important to note that a lack of self-worth, hopelessness, guilt, and bitterness is not something you just wake up with one morning. It's the culmination and conditioning of our consciousness over our entire lives. If we combine this emotional conditioning with a belief system routed in judgement and punishment, it's not entirely surprising that many of our witnesses expected to end up in Hell.

At this point you now have a good understanding of what a Hellish experience generally entails. We've read of Demons, torture, fear, taunting, the stench of Hell coupled with the hopelessness and regret of our witnesses. The following accounts will introduce experiences from witnesses that we'll refer to as 'observers'. These are witnesses that have had positive experiences, but witnessed Hell and Purgatory from afar. The problem with being in Hell, apart from the obvious pain and anguish, is that the witness is consumed by their experience. They have no objectivity; all they know is pain and hopelessness.

Observers provide context, they observe Hell for what it really is.

In any desperate situation panicking clouds our judgement and ability to understand our situation. Not panicking is easier said than done when being ripped limb from limb. However, when your mind is calm, you're able to understand and perceive the situation with more clarity. Clearly this is not an easy thing to do when you're being tortured or frozen in fear, but observers are having positive experiences. They are filled with love and security, they have universal knowledge and understanding as we've just discussed. We'll come back to why love and serenity is so important in later sections, but for now just know that an observer is able to view Hell and Purgatory objectively and is imparted with understanding of its origin and mechanics.

Few positive witnesses come back with a complete understanding of Hell, but enough have returned to give us the information we need to piece it together and answer the most important questions, "How to escape from Hell?" or more importantly, how to avoid it all together.

Wayne

In 1978 Wayne was 15 years old riding his motorcycle across a motocross track. Wayne hit a jump too fast and was thrown violently from his motorcycle hitting an upcoming jump headfirst.

"I briefly felt my heart beating, but when I opened my eyes and got up on my feet, I was shocked to be standing beside my own twisted body strewn across the ground."

"I heard a voice that I recognised but I didn't know where from. She said, 'Hurry, we must go!' When I turned to look at where this voice was coming from, I saw a glowing bright being, about the size of a young girl around six or seven years old, despite her appearance, she was strong, authoritative and firm. Shocked, I asked, 'What do you mean? Go where?' She replied in an urgent voice, 'Hurry, we must go! The dark ones are coming.' Around 60 feet away three dark figures were quickly approaching, I felt strongly they were evil tormented souls.

"I felt these evil souls were sent by Satan or another evil force. It looked like these tormented souls were tangled and rolling around themselves surrounded by a dark churning cloud. They had black clothing, white almost dead faces with

only holes for eyes. They seemed to have different feelings, I felt one was suffering pain, another was lost and consumed by its own despair and the last one was just evil and seemed to be in charge of the others as they hurtled towards me."

Wayne's experience is a departure from what we've seen so far. It would seem Wayne has a guardian angel. For positive witness's meeting a loved one, a guardian angel or a religious figure is common. There is almost always someone to guide our positive witnesses on their journey at the moment of passing. Wayne's angel refers to these tormented souls as 'the dark ones'.

He also mentions Satan, only the second time I've ever read of Satan in a witness account. However, Wayne expands on his explanation by saying, 'or another evil force'. He also speaks of these beings as being surrounded by a 'dark churning cloud'. This is the first time we've mentioned a dark cloud, but it's an incredibly important step in understanding what Hell is. Note that these beings were ALL encompassed by this dark cloud, they didn't each have a separate dark cloud surrounding each of them.

"My angel reached out to me to hold her hand, we gripped onto each other's wrists and floated up. I glanced down and saw people attending to my body, they were desperately trying to revive me. I also saw the dark ones gathered around my body, they seemed very angry that they could not have me."

This is our first witness account where a soul is saved and avoids demons or malevolent beings. Wayne is not alone, whilst many of our previous witness's escaped Hell through returning to their body, others returned via a saviour of some kind. Before we get to the specifics of leaving Hell, we'll first cover why anyone goes there in the first instance.

Preston

Preston had a run in with the law in 1995 in the early hours of the morning. As one of the perpetrators of a failed robbery, he was shot in the knee by the county sheriff, severing an artery. During Preston's lifesaving surgery he went into cardiac arrest on two occasions.

When Preston left the world of the living, he was joined by a companion that guided him through his experience. Whilst we may immediately assume that Preston is evil due to his crime, his experience clearly shows remorse.

"As I walked with my companion, we came to a valley. It stretched on as far as the eye could see. It was covered by a fog which made it hard to get a sense of the size of the valley. From the fog I could feel extraordinary sadness, I felt the sadness and started to weep."

Note how Preston is strongly affected by this sadness. In the physical world whilst we feel empathy, we rarely find ourselves weeping at the sadness of others, particularly for someone who just committed a robbery.

"The sadness felt like people wished they had done things a different way, but it was too late to change how they had lived their lives. Even so they still wished things had been different. My companion was weeping with me, we both felt a wasted life was a tragedy beyond words"

"I awoke in the ICU weeping like a child. A doctor was with me attempting to comfort me and assuring me I was okay now, she wanted to know why I was so upset. At the time I didn't know that I'd had a near death experience so told her I had a sad dream, she giggled and told me that's not possible under anaesthetic."

Preston's extraordinary empathy for the people in this fog cannot be reconciled with his actions in life. Being involved in a robbery for most people would be a terrifying experience, if Preston had the same level of empathy in life as he did in death, it's unlikely he would put people through the trauma of a robbery. This highlights the heightened emotional state witnesses have when they pass over. It also shows that Preston is not inherently a bad person, otherwise why would he feel such empathy and compassion?

Eugene

Eugene's account is short, in the late '90s he suffered an allergic reaction which led him to his experience. Whilst Eugene's account is short, it's to the point and adds a significant piece to our puzzle.

"During my experience I saw Heaven and it's opposite, Hell. The horrific torment of the people there was much worse than what we are taught, its far worse than the lakes of fire taught by preachers. It was like spending eternity in the company of others who have harmed their fellow man or forever in loneliness.

"The weird thing about this place of darkness was that it existed and didn't exist at the same time. Nobody was sent there but by themselves and by the same token only they could get themselves out. Eternity was how you wished it. Even though there were millions of souls, it was only a tiny fraction of the souls in the afterlife."

Despite Eugene's short testimony there's a huge amount of insight here. As an observer he did not enter Hell, he merely passed over it. He witnessed some of the horrific acts of torture we've already discussed and observed Purgatory.

Eugene does however make some contradicting statements; he says souls are 'spending eternity in the company of others who have harmed their fellow man' whilst paradoxically saying 'nobody was sent there but by themselves'. This would imply that people are condemned but have the choice to 'un-condemn' themselves. Based on what you've read about Hell so far, would you willingly choose to be condemned in such a place?

On the face of it, this contradiction may seem as though Eugene is not being completely honest with us, when in actual fact, he's just misinterpreted the situation. The most important observation Eugene has made is that the souls in Hell and Purgatory have chosen, albeit inadvertently, to be there. He says that, "Eternity was how you wished it" and "only they could get themselves out," but what does he mean by this? How exactly does a tortured soul get out of Hell? To get answers, we need more information.

Samantha

In 1989 Samantha was cycling home from a volunteering position. As she approached a traffic light, she was struck by a truck. Her injuries were comprehensive; collapsed lungs, extensive organ damage, a broken pelvis, and several broken ribs. Fortunately for Samantha a police officer was nearby and came to her aid, otherwise we may never of had the opportunity to hear her story. We join Samantha midway through her experience.

"I found myself flying over a place that resembled a classical Hell. It was filled with screams of agonising pain and suffering. Naked people were strewn over a wasteland with pools of boiling excrement and jagged rocks. Demons and animals were torturing people in all manner of ways, and people were torturing each other.

"As I neared this place, I felt a pulling sensation drawing me in but instead flew over this miserable landscape. The smell was putrid whilst the heat was almost unbearable. I was captivated by the infinite ways beings were inflicting pain and anguish on the inhabitants of this place. I felt I wanted to leave so had no problem leaving and felt that no one or

nothing was holding those people there in captivity except their belief in their agony and continued suffering."

There are similarities between Eugene's and Samantha's accounts. Eugene stated, "Nobody was sent there but by themselves" whilst Samantha says, "Nothing was holding those people there in captivity except their belief in their agony and continued suffering." This is quite the dilemma, again, why would anyone believe in their own agony or want eternal suffering and torture?

"The next place in the tunnel wasn't much better.
"As far as the eye could see, there were people walking along a yellow barren land. Their heads were tilted down, they were completely mesmerised in their own miserable wallowing thoughts completely unaware of the other people that shuffled along beside them. I felt an overwhelming sense of loneliness and isolation coming from this place."

Samantha's experience is insightful, she observes both classical Hell and Purgatory. We again hear of the putrid smell, the torture, and the demons. We learn that souls can somehow choose to leave Hell but it's not clear how. If it was simply a case of taking the exit, surely everyone would be rushing out of Hell.

It's difficult with only Samantha and Eugene's account to unravel this mystery just yet, but our next witness account fills in the blanks and starts to paint a picture that we can start to understand.

Justin

It was whilst I was reading this account that the pieces of the puzzle started to come together, I had numerous and profound light bulb moments. Could I have stumbled across the answer to Hell? We've discussed the phenomenon of instantaneous understanding. This means for people such as Justin, they are able to understand what they observe without any verbal explanation.

Justin is from the United Kingdom, his experience occurred in 2004 after a critical car accident, he remained undiscovered for five hours immediately after the accident. Justin fell into a coma for seven days following his accident.

Justin's account is extensive, which I'm incredibly grateful for, but we're going to focus on what he saw on Earth. We start with Justin observing Earth high above the ground looking down on the people and souls of Earth.

"Seeing the earth, I became aware of several things. I could see many other spirits, beings, who were also leaving their bodies and moving away from the Earth. However, many of them in their spiritual bodies seemed to not be able to see the light and love above. They had almost like clouds above

their heads, like clouds blocking out the sun, it's still there but we can't see it."

Justin's experience is extraordinary, not only does he observe souls leaving Earth, of which there are approximately 100,000 per day, but he also discerns clouds above the heads of many souls. He continues to describe the mechanics of these clouds.

"I was very aware that those clouds were their thought and feeling patterns, the more angry, hateful, bitter, etc., the bigger and darker these clouds, which is just another description for their minds. The more negative ones also seemed to be looking down not even up. I could experience their feelings, anger, etc. I wanted them to look up and see the love and come to the light, but I couldn't get my message to them. This is part of the experience that is not nice."

Justin understands that these clouds are blocking out the light and love above. The light and love Justin describes is Heaven and God. Whilst many witnesses have different descriptions of Heaven according to which part of Heaven they visited, light and love is consistent in every account.

Just because a person has feelings of anger and bitterness, it doesn't mean they are going to Hell. Many positive witnesses describe feelings of hate or anger at the moment of death while still experiencing Heaven.

Note that Justin is able to identify the direction the souls are looking; this indicates they retain human form. We've touched on this before, Hellish witnesses retain their human form. Our Hellish witnesses have described their limbs being torn off, or their hair being ripped out. In Heaven we have no physical form unless we wish it. This is a clue as to the progression of the soul through the afterlife. As we come closer to God, we shed our human form, because we let go of our lives and return to Heaven in our soul form. For Hell and Purgatory, we haven't truly let go of our lives. We hold onto the toxic attitudes and emotions that come with it, so we are not able to fully free ourselves of our mortal body, even if it's just a shadow of our mortal lives.

"Those negative beings seemed to come from the Earth and go down away from the light, I was aware of them going to a void/darkness/suffering or perpetual round and round in circles in their experiences/mind of the negative record player almost habits of thoughts and feelings. I was aware of them going somewhere like Hell, but I was not allowed to remember it, or it has been blocked from my memory. The love and light didn't want them to experience that and was doing all it could to let them come to it. But they could not or would not accept or see it."

Justin notes that these souls are going down to Hell.

He cannot elaborate on the details of Hell because his knowledge and memories of Hell have been taken from him. This is not uncommon, many witnesses describe learning of profound and fundamental knowledge, but the knowledge is taken from them when they return. They remember knowing something important and they know it was taken from them. In many cases it is explained to them why they will not be permitted to remember. The reasons include having knowledge that could detrimentally affect the fate of man, knowledge that could harm their own lives in some way, or knowledge humanity is not ready to receive.

"It was obvious they were creating this experience, not a separate devil or God punishing them. Maybe their life review filled them with so much remorse they had to punish themselves. Maybe in the life review they did not feel any remorse and just felt anger at when others had felt good in their suffering or downfall."

Justin mentions the Life Review. We'll discuss the Life Review in much more detail later. The Life Review can be a contentious subject, I've had many intense debates on this. When you hear someone say, "My life flashed before my eyes," it's likely this phrase came from the more comprehensive Life Review. During the Life Review you literally relive your entire life from birth. Key moments are picked out, these include moments where you have shown love and kindness, but also moments where you have shown hate, anger or hurt another person. During the Life Review you will experience every kind and loving emotion you've shared, whilst at the same time you will experience the pain and suffering you've inflicted on others, you will, for all intense purposes, 'be that person'. The part people struggle with is the concept that this is not God judging people, it's the culmination of our entire life where the intent is for us to learn from our experiences, good and bad. During our Life Review we are joined by God or another loving soul to guide us through this experience, to embrace us when we are riddled with shame and guilt and to rejoice with us when we show compassion, love and kindness.

Justin states clearly that these souls were creating this experience themselves, it wasn't God or a devil of some kind. This is sensitive subject, the concept of judgement and punishment from God, but as I've stated many times, I've never read a credible witness account that included any judgment from God, or any other being in the afterlife. Justin describes that souls in Hell may not have been able to complete their life review or show remorse for their actions, and this is why they are in Hell. He clearly states that God did not send these souls to Hell, it was because they were unable to process their Life Review and ultimately condemned themselves to Hell.

There is no place in Heaven for hate and anger, but equally, you would not be cast out by God. This subject is more complicated than it would appear on the surface. Our souls natural state is not hatred, anger or evil. It is love, unity, compassion, and acceptance. Any hateful feelings we harbour are exclusively the product of our experiences on Earth.

Whilst I disagree with some of the teachings from scripture, such as a judgement, division and punishment, there are some critical concepts of Christianity (and other religions) that are vitally important to our afterlife journey. Forgiveness is a cornerstone of Christianity, but it's not just for the benefit of the aggressor. Hate is a heavy burden on anyone, it eats away at our mental wellness. By forgiving others we also relieve ourselves of the hate and contempt we hold in our psyche, we free up that space in my mind to focus on more positive things, instead of focusing on painful feelings such as loss and hatred. There are many cases where a family has forgiven the crime of a perpetrator against them. They do this for themselves because they know that carrying that hate will never help them heal. For the rest of us, we could never imagine forgiving a heinous crime such as murder, but remember, hate is hate no matter what form it takes, and no matter the justification for that hate, nothing good will ever come of it. We could say that evil is the absence of love.

During the Life Review, which we'll cover extensively later, if we are unable to forgive ourselves for the hate and pain we've inflicted on Earth, it will burden and ultimately pull us away from the light.

"I do know though that it was their choice, their creation, not a separate God's choice or devil. I never experienced any type of separate devil or being calling them. They just could not see the light their minds/hearts were obstructed by their current and past thoughts, habits, it was there so bright and obvious to me but they just could not see it. Maybe it was where I was going or what I experienced in the beginning when in the void and seemed aware of some negative entities/beings. I am no saint and have done much wrong in my life, so I do not understand still why I was never like that myself."

Despite Justin's newfound understanding of the universe, he cannot fathom why he was able to see the light, whilst all these other poor souls could not. This gets to the route of why Justin's experience is so important. I mentioned earlier that souls in Hell cannot be objective because they are consumed by their fear and negative emotions. Justin's experience eventually brought him a view of Earth, but he did mention feeling some negative entities in the Void, or Nexus as we've called it. Most humans harbour some negative emotion, whether it's guilt, sadness, or something more sinister, such as hatred and bitterness. It is to be expected that most souls will have this 'dark cloud' over their heads when they cross over, but that doesn't mean they will retain it. Once they are in the presence of absolute unconditional love and acceptance, for most of us, these feelings will quickly disappear.

Even the Nexus is a place of calm and tranquillity for most souls where witnesses describe losing all sense of fear and any other negative emotion, thereby shedding their 'dark cloud'. Justin most likely did have his own 'dark cloud' at the moment of his crossing, but it dissipated once his journey progressed, and by the time he found his way back to Earth as our observer, that dark cloud had completely left him. Another reason Justin may have avoided Hell is that he had already learnt and grown from his misdeeds. I have read witness accounts where the Life Review was entirely positive, despite the witness having shown hate and anger towards others in their life on Earth, but they had learnt and grown from those experiences so there was no value in reliving that which you've already learnt from.

"Some were coming to the light or looking up had no dark swirling or just a bit of energy above and around their heads. But from what I remember, only a really small percentage maybe one in a hundred or less."

On the face of it, this may seem like distressing information. Justin is telling us that only around one in a hundred didn't have a 'dark cloud'. It comes back to what we've already covered, almost all humans will have some form of negative emotion at the time of passing, and that's okay. For most of us, we struggle with our negative emotions in one way or another, whether it's depression, anger, guilt, or envy most of us have some form of negativity in our hearts. But there will always be a small number of people on Earth who are completely at peace with themselves. It doesn't mean they are better than you or me, it just means they show love to others in their lives, or they have learnt from their mistakes and become better people. They've managed to find a way to live where they harbour no ill feelings, they are content. For most of us mere humans this is an unattainable or impractical way of life. For everyone else, we all carry a 'dark cloud' over us. We're only human at the end of the day.

As I've already mentioned, our natural state is not hatred, it's love. Our 'dark cloud' is the vessel for all of the negative emotions and feelings we've collected throughout our life, it cannot be a part of our souls because our souls do not contain evil, and so it hangs over our souls until we let it go.

"I became aware too, of beings, mainly human on the Earth, still alive, and could again see this either clearness or light about them or dark swirling thoughts energy. Again very, very few seemed to be positive. A few, a couple in each continent, seemed to be material form and able to see the light whilst alive, they were looking up smiling aware of it with no dark negative thoughts/energies around them, maybe ten or twenty in the whole world. The rest of humanity had a mixture, but most were looking down and had much darkness about them."

Justin tells us that most people on Earth were looking down. This doesn't mean they were looking down to Hell, it just means they are not looking up to God, or the light. We've already discussed the rise in an agnostic way of life, so it's not entirely surprising that people are further away from the light.

We'll come back to the implications of Justin's experience shortly, but first there are some important things you need to know.

Agape, the Force of Love

Pronounced 'Ah-gah-pay'.

You've heard the term 'love' used a lot in the preceding pages. It's important I explain what I mean by 'love'. It's not like the love between a husband or wife, or even the love between a mother and child. It's stronger than that, it's more like a force than a feeling. In ancient Greek there is a word that describes this love, '*Agape*'. Agape is described as the following.

'The highest form of love, charity' and *'the love of God for man and of man for God'*.

It's easy to roll your eyes and shrug this off as some sort of hippy notion or religious fanaticism, but it's important you understand what Agape is, and why it's so fundamental to everything. A good analogy would be the famous 'force' from the Star Wars franchise. It's actually similar in many ways. The force of love, or Agape, is a powerful force that permutates through everything in the universe, just like the force in Star Wars. It is an energy that connects everything, it is the fuel that powers your soul, the Heavens and it is the rejection of this force that allows Hell to exist.

Despite the Greeks developing a word to describe this force of love, the majority of NDE witnesses struggle to find words to describe it.

"There are no words in the human language to describe the feeling of warmth, belonging, peace, and especially love. Euphoria is a word that comes to mind, however, it still does no justice explaining the feeling. The word love does no justice either, for we think we know what love is, such as the love a mother has for a newborn child. Multiply that by thousands, and we might come close; if not, at least we would find ourselves headed in the right direction." – Charles, 1992

"They overwhelmed us with a feeling of the highest love & compassion that was well beyond anything we could experience on Earth." – Will, 2010

"All I remember was a beautiful white bright light, and the overwhelming feeling of love and acceptance. I felt like this was the best feeling I could ever have asked for. I have never felt that kind of love before or since. I knew there was someone/something there with me." – Tony, 2008

"As I got further is when I had the overwhelming sense of my body absorbing all of this light, it engulfed me, it washed me, it filled me up with such love I cannot explain there is no word stronger than love here on earth to describe it." – Kim, 2005

"This light contained overwhelming love, more love and beauty than I can express." – Guy, 1990

"I felt absolute comfort and love there, like I have never felt before." – Lisa, 2010

"I came to know that love is a power to rival all powers real and perceived in the universe, something I never could have understood without this experience." – Ally, 1976

You can see from our witness's statements, this force is more than just a feeling, it goes beyond words, beyond description. It's hard for those of us who haven't experienced an NDE to appreciate Agape. With the exception of distressing and Hellish NDE's, pretty much every person that has an NDE has experienced this force of love. For the rest of us we can only dream of the day we get to bask in this inexplicable feeling.

Your Powerful Soul

We, our souls, are powerful beings. As we live our lives and become more connected and grounded to the physical realities of our physical world, we begin to lose our connection to the light and to each other. This is why Justin saw so many dark clouds and so many people looking away from the light.

When we pass to the other side, this power is activated. This includes a heightened emotional state, a deep connection with the universe, instantaneous understanding, and things we have not yet covered, such as the ability to instantly travel anywhere in the Universe and to other realms of reality. The source of this power we've already discussed, Agape. A mechanic of this power is the 'Law of Attraction'. Wikipedia describes the 'Law of Attraction' as:

"In the New Thought philosophy, the Law of Attraction is the belief that positive or negative thoughts bring positive or negative experiences into a person's life. The belief is based on the ideas that people and their thoughts are made from 'pure energy', and that a process of like energy attracting like energy exists through which a person can improve their health, wealth, and personal relationships."

Only the concept from the theory of the Law of Attraction is relevant to our journey, and our interpretation. Let's make some modifications to Wikipedia's description:

"The Law of Attraction is the belief that positive or negative thoughts and emotions bring positive or negative experiences into a person's life. The belief is based on the ideas that people's thoughts and emotions are made from 'pure energy', and that a process of like energy attracting like energy exists."

I can't speak to the Law of Attraction having some kind of impact on the physical world, or a person's Earthly life. The concept that 'like energy attracts like energy' is, however, on the money. We are only concerned with the attraction of energy to energy, specifically the energy of Agape. The opposite of Agape is hatred, bitterness, fear, guilt, and all other negative emotions, which also have their own energy.

At the time of our passing, when we leave our physical bodies, our souls are freed from their Earthly shackles. We revert to our pure soul form. At this point we are pure energy; we retain our consciousness and memories of our lives. The only thing we take with us after death is our consciousness, emotions, and knowledge, and it is in this form that our feelings and emotions are absolutely fundamental to where we go next.

As our witnesses have stated, Hell is of your own creation, or more specifically Hell is of 'our' own creation. Going to Hell is, however, entirely your own decision, albeit subconsciously. There is one more concept I need to introduce you to in order to understand why Hell exists, how it persists and why anyone would choose to end up in this horrific place.

Ancient Egregore

This is the most important concept in this entire book. It's why Hell exists, it's why it persists and it's why any soul would go there. I'd already drawn my conclusions on the mechanics of Hell before I came across a word that describes it. It was during my research that I discovered this word, or concept. I posed a question regarding the negative dark clouds we discussed to a network of NDErs:

"Have any NDErs observed 'dark clouds' with negative feelings or emotions floating over the heads of other people/souls at the beginning of your journey to Heaven or at any point during your NDE? Or have you witnessed or observed a large/vast dark cloud or fog of negative emotion/feelings during your experience?"

The first response asks me:

"Why do you ask this? Was this what happened to you? I read about this description in a book. The author called it Egregore, but I think it's a well-known concept. Maybe you could start your search with this concept on the internet."

Immediately, my internet search confirmed this is indeed the correct term to describe the mechanics of Hell.

"Egregore is an occult concept representing a 'thoughtform' or 'collective group mind', an autonomous psychic entity made up of, and influencing, the thoughts of a group of people."

As we've already discussed, Wikipedia takes a very matter of fact to approach to everything. Whilst this is a short summary is does highlight some important points. An Egregore is autonomous, meaning it exists independently of some external control or force. This entity is made up of people's thoughts but is powered by their emotions. An incredibly important point of the Egregore is that it influences the thoughts of those that inhabit it.

We've come across Egregores in Earth's history with horrific and devastating consequences. The best example of this is the Egregore created by Adolf Hitler. Through his rhetoric and nationalistic speeches Hitler was able to convince an entire nation that murder, and persecution was in the service of some higher order, and therefore was acceptable. It's likely had Hitler never had come into the lives of the German people at the time, they would never have endorsed such ideology. The power of the Egregore twisted what is normally considered unacceptable and turned regular people into complicit war criminals.

Nations from around the world looked on in astonishment and horror whilst other leaders became attracted to this nationalistic fascist ideal, and ultimately followed suit. In World War II there were two distinct Egregores, the Allies and the Axis powers. Their values could not be more opposing, nations rallied around freedom versus other nations that desired oppression. Just as the Germans, Italians and Japanese were swept away by their Egregore, so to were the Western powers in their pursuit of opposing values, such as freedom and liberty.

The word 'Egregore' originally derives from the Greek word *Egrégoroi* meaning 'watchers'. It appears in the Septuagint translation of the Book of Lamentations, the Book of Jubilees and the Book of Enoch going as far back as the third and fourth century BC. Similar concepts were mentioned in the Dead Sea Scrolls. These historic documents mention Egregores as both good and evil angels, or watchers, but largely focus on the fallen and rebellious angels. The concept of an Egregore becoming a collective thought-form was first introduced by the 'Rosicrucianism' spiritual and cultural movement in the seventeenth century AD. The famous Masonic Philosophical Society, or Masons, also studied Egregore's summarising the phenomenon as "a group mind which is created when people consciously (or unconsciously) come together for a common purpose."

The majority of descriptions of an Egregore focus on positive aspects of the phenomenon. If we take a look at another description of an Egregore, we can start to build the connection to a more sinister manifestation of this collective state of mind or thought form.

"Any symbolic pattern that has served as a focus for human emotion and energy will build up an egregore of its own over time, and the more energy that is put into such a

pattern, the more potent the egregore that will form around it." – Source, Theosophy Wiki

Egregores can also be described as their own entity, almost like a living organism of energy. The energy within the Egregore can be experienced by all the individuals contributing to its existence, either for or against their will.

Our Hell

We already know that our souls are beings of pure emotional energy and their natural state is fuelled by Agape, or the force of love. As we live our lives, we collect negative emotions, characteristics and feelings that form the dark clouds observed by Justin. When we pass to the afterlife, we cannot take our negative emotional energy to Heaven, as we've already discussed there is no place for rage, hate, guilt and bitterness in Heaven. For most of us, our balance of negative emotion versus our inherent positive emotion allows us to shed our dark cloud and ascend to Heaven. For those of us that harbour deep rage and resentment towards others, their dark cloud will be denser and more integrated into their consciousness.

Unlike Heaven, where God is the custodian and the source of divine love or Agape, of which all souls were created, Hell is a human creation. It's the exception to Heaven. As Eugene stated in our earlier account.

"The weird thing about this place of darkness was that it existed and didn't exist at the same time. Nobody was sent there but by themselves and by the same token only they could

get themselves out. Eternity was how you wished it." –
Eugene, 1999

Heaven is not a collective thought-form, it is the kingdom of God, and ultimately our 'home'. It has structure, places, and things beyond our wildest imagining. Hell, on the other hand, is not a kingdom or a place, it is a mass of negative emotional energy and human manifestation. The Law of Attraction states that 'like energy is attracted to like energy' and so it stands that souls who enter the afterlife consumed by negative emotional energy are attracted to, and add to, this negative Egregore, or as it is more commonly known, Hell. This ancient Egregore contains the collective minds of billions of souls going back thousands of years, their experiences, their beliefs, and their desperation.

Inside an Egregore, the individuals fuelling it add their own unique selves to it. This is why so many Hellish witnesses experience what I've described as 'traditional Hell'. Fire, anti-religious symbols, demons based on mythology and theology, torment and earthly torture are all human creations. Hell is the collective preconceptions of those that have created it through their predetermined interpretations and beliefs going back thousands of years, perhaps hundreds of thousands of years.

Preconceptions of reoccurring themes from newly added souls reinforce certain Hellish concepts, such as demons and torture. The physical aspects described by witnesses are manifestations of their own preconceptions of Hell, combined with the manifestations from other souls within the Egregore. No single soul controls the Egregore. It's reinforced by every soul within it, hence the chaos of Hell.

Because each soul is a part of a wider collective thought-form, the overall manifestation becomes a single shared experience with some unique aspects according to the individual experiencing it. This ultimately results in Hell becoming a physical place to those that exist within it. From the outside, if we were to visualise it, it might look like an immense swirling dark electrical storm cloud, just as some of our witnesses have described it. Some witnesses, particularly those that have resorted to suicide, describe a dark cloud or fog descending on them at the time of death. There are some interesting accounts of dark clouds mentioned in several witness accounts.

In 1980 Agustin recounted a dark cloud during his NDE when he suffered a cardiac arrest from a fatal allergic reaction to penicillin.

"I soon found myself in a space and place unknown to me, having arrived there at a velocity I was unfamiliar with, with a force of attraction like that of metal to a magnet. I entered a place where it started to turn dark as if I was inside a cloud, and it was becoming denser and darker, and in that darkness, which became almost total, I glimpsed a tiny star or light, which, from the exact time I noticed it, attracted me without hesitation towards it."

Witnesses consistently mention a feeling of a magnet, being compelled, or pulled towards something. As we know, magnets are an attracting force, so this aligns with the mechanics of our Egregore. Agustin mentions that he was inside a dark cloud but soon passed through it and was instead attracted to the light. We can surmise, based on what we've discussed so far, that Augustin's emotional truth is not of a negative nature and therefore he simply passes through the dark cloud and onto the light. He never merges or becomes part of it.

Other witnesses have specifically described this dark cloud as evil. In Gregg's account in 1975 he was imparted with knowledge of the future. Seeing aspects of the future during an NDE is incredibly common, typically it's the future of the witness, but in many cases, it can be the future of humanity.

"I saw a large dark cloud engulfing the Earth in twenty or more years from now? I couldn't see clearly what it was, but it felt very powerful and very evil indeed."

Gregg's account was in 1975 whilst Justin's account was in 2004, some 29 years later. Justin described seeing clouds throughout the Earth in the present, while Gregg saw a vision of the future. These two completely unrelated accounts appear to seemingly validate each other. I don't think Gregg's vision meant the end of the world, just an increase in humanity losing sight of the light, and an increase in negative emotions between people throughout the world. We've certainly seen that throughout 2020.

Authors of NDE experiences have also mentioned dark clouds in their books. Dr Rajiv Parti, former chief of anaesthesiology at Bakersfield Heart Hospital, had an experience featured on Time.com that he included in his book *Dying to Wake Up*. In his experience he described the following:

"Then fear overcame him when his awareness drifted to a place where a great, wildfire was raging. He could see lightning in dark clouds and smell the odour of burning meat. He said he realised that an unseen force was pulling him into Hell, leaving him in the midst of souls who were screaming and suffering."

Dr Parti's account fits with our other witness account. The smell of burning meat, the screaming and suffering. Notice how Dr Parti speaks of how the dark cloud pulled him into Hell, again we are back to this magnetic attracting force. This is why I believe the Law of Attraction is fundamental to the afterlife, and to our transition to the other side. Dr Parti also personally witnesses the Egregore of Hell with lightning striking through dark clouds.

Demons

So how do we explain the behaviour of the beings that exist in Hell? Why are they so desperate to inflict pain on others? Why are there demons at all? Why do some demons form groups?

It's important to note the souls that exist in Hell do not know they are contributing to their own damnation; they are unaware they are the architects of their own prison. An Egregore does not imply order, many of our witness's describe chaos because that's all there is. The souls in this place are afraid, confused, full of resentment, anger, rage, and hatred. These negative feelings are reinforced by the Egregore and its inhabitants. Only chaos and madness can reign under such conditions, and whilst the souls here have intelligence, they are primeval and animalistic. The torment that defines Hell has existed there from the moment it was formed because it was this very emotional torment that created it in the first place. The human instinct to survive no doubt kicks in, such as a grouping with other tormented souls and following some form of command structure.

We can only begin to imagine the psychology of such a place. To what lengths will immortal humans go under such extraordinary and horrific circumstances, over an extended period of time, perhaps hundreds or thousands of years. It's possible a soul may try to avoid its own torment by tormenting others, a kind of mob mentality, which coincidentally is a form of earthly Egregore.

It's unlikely the souls that inhabit Hell know the mechanics of its energy, they are just compelled to continue feeding it hatred, rage, contempt, and suffering. Extended exposure within Hell most likely completely consumes its inhabitants to the point where they absorb the hatred, desperation and ultimately the evil from the other souls that exist there.

Demons are a consistent theological subject of religion, many souls that enter Hell will have had preconceptions of demons and other Hellish themes in their earthly lives. When these souls enter Hell, they bring with them these preconceptions. Because an Egregore is a thought-form, not a physical entity, demons are manifestations of the tormented souls. The variety of demonic forms is the product of various preconceptions of suffering and torment through the ages. The desire to inflict pain and suffering on others coupled with the Egregore's amplification of collective negative energy explains why souls would take on demonic forms. If a soul was bent on inflicting suffering and torment, what could be more frightening than a twisted creature with horns and fangs,

Demons are the ultimate nightmarish creatures. It may not be a conscious decision for a human to take a demonic form. If a soul found themselves in Hell due to the guilt they found in their Life Review, its plausible they would perceive themselves as a monster, and as such manifest such an appearance.

Hell is an ancient Egregore, souls absorbed by it would have lived in a time where Hell and damnation was widely believed to be most people's fate. The negative emotional energy of Hell influences its inhabitants, so even if a soul enters Hell with the best of intentions, eventually they would likely succumb to its influence and so the perpetual cycle of evil continues.

Does this mean that anyone with negative emotion is destined for Hell? No, it does not. Many witness accounts include people going to Heaven after attempting suicide, harbouring negative emotions due to a life of trauma, or resenting God due to suffering they've experienced in life. We do not know exactly why some witnesses experience Hellish NDE's when the vast majority of NDE's are positive. Barbara Rommer authored a book published in 2000 which includes some fascinating facts into the percentages of those that suffer from Hellish, or distressing NDE's. In Barbara's research she determined that 55% of distressing experiences were attributed to self-induced death, or suicide. Of that 55%, 18% reported a Hellish NDE involving traditional Hell and demons.

NDE's can be distressing even when they don't involve suffering, demons, and torture. For example, witnesses find themselves in dark desolate places of nothingness. Whilst this is not as horrific as traditional Hell, it is still destressing to the witness.

Most suicide NDE reports that Barbara studied were of positive experiences. She also discovered that witnesses who expected some form of judgement or punishment also had a positive NDE.

It's impossible for us to completely understand the complexities of Hell and why some people go there whilst others do not. Far more research is required for us to build a more comprehensive picture. But all of our witnesses have returned from Hell, or gone to an altogether different place, and it's from their testimony that we can build an interpretation and connect the dots. We may not know everything, but in the oasis of witness reports we have access to, there are insights that can lead us in the right direction.

Whilst I cannot give you an exhaustive list of negative emotions that are attracted to Hell, I can pick out ones that overwhelmingly stand out among Hellish experiences, guilt. Whilst Barbara Rommer's research determined that many witnesses who expected some form of punishment or judgement did not have Hellish experiences, it's likely their expectation was based on a belief system, not an emotional truth. For example, they have been told there is punishment and judgement based on their religious learnings, and as a result they expect some form of religious judgement or punishment. On the other hand, if you've spent your entire life feeling like a failure and undeserving of love, this is an ingrained emotional truth that defines you and your actions through your life. It is a part of who you are.

An Egregore cannot be tricked. You can say that you believe you should be judged and punished, but if you do not truly feel this way and have not led a life that reflects this truth, you will not be attracted to it. Of course none of our witnesses specifically said they want to go to Hell, that would be insane, but some believed they were destined for Hell and therefore had made the unconscious decision to go there.

Remember, an Egregore is a manifestation created by humans, but it does not have some independent sentient power that allows it to take people or souls into its midst by force. It must be a conscious or subconscious decision.

Teaching us that unless we behave in a certain way, or worship a certain deity, we will ultimately end up in Hell could potentially be one of the contributing factors that nudges us there. If you're religious and feel as though you are failing your religion, or you are failing God, which then leads to a prolonged feeling of guilt and a lack of self-worth through a large portion of your life, this could ultimately result in you ending up in Hell.

Aside from negative emotions that are attracted to Hell, the lack of a positive emotion can also attract us to Hell. That emotion is love, and this time I am talking about the love between a husband and wife, or a mother and child. Love erodes Hell. Whilst Earthly love does not compare to God's love, it is still love and as we've already discussed, evil is the absence of love. God is pure love, or Agape, and all other forms of love are ultimately a part of God's love.

If you take anything from this book, regardless of what you believe, just remember that you are not evil and you belong in Heaven, it is quite literally your *home*. You do not deserve Hell. You were created from love and your soul is filled with it. There is nothing you can do in life that damns you to Hell. You will have to face your deeds, good and bad, when your time on this Earth ends, but it will not be God judging you, you will be judging yourself. That's not to say the Life Review will be smooth sailing for most of us. I've heard terms such as shame, intense guilt and embarrassment used whilst describing the Life Review. As you might expect, witnesses are humbled in God's presence, and so during the Life Review even though we are embraced and comforted by God or another divine guardian, we feel ashamed at every act of indifference, contempt or pain we have inflicted on others.

God's love for you is profound, he feels your pain, he lives with you through your torment and he weeps with you when you suffer. God does not have favourites, despite what some religions will teach you, he loves us all equally with no judgement. He has always only wanted what is best for you. This may be getting a bit preachy now, but I assure you this is what you need to know when your time comes. Even if you Don't believe it now, my hope is that you'll remember it when you need it. Take your guilt and shame, learn from it, and move on.

To reinforce this message, here's an extract from Sarah's experience. Sarah was abused both emotionally and physically as a child. At the age of 14 she was injured, during surgery she lost consciousness. Like so many children, Sarah blamed herself for her abuse. During her experience, her spiritual companion answers her questions.

"I wanted to be good all the time so no one was mad at me. And I seem to always mess up and I didn't want God to be mad at me. He said, 'There is nothing you could do that could ever change the way God feels about you.' He said God loves me. I said, 'He does?' He said, 'Yes, He does.' I said, 'I wish I was special, like the people in the Bible.' He said, 'You are.'"

Kerry also believes she does not deserve the love of God. In 2015 Kerry suffered an allergic reaction leading to cardiac arrest. The way others have treated her throughout her life has carved a feeling of rejection into her emotional truth.

"I was thinking, 'Was this the Lake of Fire moment? Would I be cast into Hell for being an abomination?' With absolute humility, I uttered seven words, 'I'm gay, will you still love me?'

"As God brought me in for a Cosmic Hug, He said, 'You are my child. I love you. I love you. I love you. Go tell 'em.' He said it with a Southern accent. He patted me on the back like a coach encouraging his player to get back in the game."

Romans 10:13 Whoever Calls on the Name of the Lord Shall Be Saved

It's time to complete the stories of our witnesses that found themselves in Hell. I mentioned various times that many of our witness's experiences went in an entirely altogether different direction. We'll now wrap up those stories and find out how our witnesses escaped from Hell.

We've determined from Justin's experience that most of us on Earth carry negative energy which is manifested as a dark cloud that hangs over us. We know that Hell is an Egregore formed over thousands of years, and that this negative energy such as hatred, guilt, rage, and bitterness are attracted to this Egregore. Understanding the mechanics of this doesn't diminish the horror of Hell. The power of the souls that inhabit Hell are able to manifest a reality that is all too real to those that are bound by it, knowing how it works doesn't make it any less horrific.

We talked about how to avoid Hell through the understanding that we all deserve Heaven, that there is nothing we can do that will make God love us less. We are only human and make mistakes, and the most important thing is to learn from those mistakes, and not to be consumed by our guilt. To value ourselves, and to value all others.

However, despite all of this, there are those of us who cannot move past our guilt, cynicism, anger, and hatred for others, or ourselves. There will also be those of us that cannot complete our Life Review due to the pain we have inflicted on others, unable to live through the suffering we have placed upon others. We'll cover the Life Review in extensive detail after this chapter.

Jim's Saviour

We left Jim's account with demons telling him, "We told you already that this is your heaven, and we are your God," whilst he was being tortured, not much of a happy ending. Jim's experience continues.

"At the time I don't know why I started doing this, but I just started saying prayer out loud, even though I was atheist, I said, 'The lord is my shepherd, I should not want, he make me lay down in green pastures, for his namesake.' I kept repeating this over and over, the creatures at first stopped feeding on me, one of them said praying won't help but I carried on anyway. They became agitated, curled up and started screaming at me, 'No one is coming for you!' I tried different prayers, this time I said, 'Yea, I walk through the valley of the shadow of death, I will fear no evil for thou are with me, thy staff and thy rod. They comfort me.'"

Jim's demons are clearly becoming distressed.

Despite Jim not being religious, he is reciting prayer. The words are unimportant, it's the intent and acknowledgement that matters. Jim continues with his prayer.

"I was compelled to keep praying, I knew I was in Hell and so with what little strength and will I had remaining I kept on praying, 'He leadeth me beside the still waters and he restored my soul. You set a table before in the face of my enemies, You pour oil over my head and over flow my soul, Your love and kind have always been with me.' It was this moment that I had a wonderous feeling come over me. I suddenly heard someone speak to me, 'Jim, open your eyes, it's me.' I recognised the voice, it was a girl I was into when I was younger, she died in an air accident back in 2003. She spoke to someone else who was with us, 'He's too afraid to open his eyes, Sandra, maybe you can help him.' And then I heard a voice and I knew it was my mom, she said, 'Jim, my beautiful thanksgiving baby boy, your safe now, please open your eyes, baby.' I knew it was my mum because she was the only one that called me thanksgiving baby, I was born on thanksgiving.

"I did eventually open my eyes and saw my mum standing in front of me, she hugged and told me to look down. I saw that my body was whole again, everything was back the way it should be."

Whilst Jim's salvation was through prayer, as you'll see in the following pages, he could have been saved in any number of ways. Remember what Justin witnessed, it was the inability for souls to see the light and thus they were attracted to the darkness. The light was always there waiting for them, but they couldn't see it. By Jim praying he opened his eyes to the light and was ultimately saved by it.

Mandy's Saviour

We left Mandy's story whilst she was being pursued by dark shadows when a voice asked her, *"Mandy, what do you know to be true of Jesus Christ?" I answered, 'That he died on the cross for me.'"* Mandy's story continues.

"All of sudden a light shot through the darkness. A hand stretched out taking mine. I floated upwards, I felt like a young child becoming a beautiful woman as I ascended, I was whole, healed and I was in the company of God. I felt such love that it made me giddy like a schoolgirl.

"In all this love and joy a voice cried out, 'Somebody help me!' I knew instantly it was my husband. My heart ached and I thought to myself I cannot leave him like that, suddenly I felt a great weight and I was back in my body."

Mandy's salvation differs from Jim's, her saviour reached out to her and she answered. Whilst we cannot explain why, it would appear that souls in an Egregore can be reached once they acknowledge the light, be it God, Jesus or any other being of light. This tells us that beings of light can literally reach into Hell and pull tormented souls out into the light.

Rachel's Saviour

We left Rachel at the moment she'd accepted that Purgatory was her eternal prison. We spoke about how the absence of love can feed the Egregore of Hell. Love is an opposing force to Hell. In the continuation of Rachel's story, we see how important love truly is.

"I believed I would spend the rest of eternity in this dark empty place replaying in my head what a stupid mistake it was to inhale the nitrous. I completely failed my daughter and family. I was sad but I knew what I had done wrong and understood I could have done better. As soon as I felt remorse for my actions, I heard a voice. I didn't recognise whose voice it was, they said, 'You don't belong here. You need to find something in life that you love and get out.'

I instantly thought of my daughter and shouted, 'Susie! I love Susie!' Next, I was lying on the floor, one of the party goers was on top of me performing chest compressions. He looked straight into my eyes and told me, 'I felt the flames.'"

This is not the first time we've seen someone in the physical world share a witness's Hellish experience.

Mandy's husband heard audible sounds from Hell, whereas one of Rachel's friends physically felt flames from Rachel's experience. Rachel was able to see the light through the Egregores influence by recalling her love for her child. We've already spoken about how love erodes Hell. This explains how Rachel was able to connect with the light. Like Mandy, Rachel had a saviour too, but she only heard from her saviour once she acknowledged, or learnt, from her mistake.

Cindy's Saviour

We left Cindy in Purgatory, she was screaming for God over and over. Cindy told us during her testimony that God was not with her, it's more likely she's just couldn't see God.

"After screaming for God's help again and again, a giant hand suddenly descended on me and pulled me from the darkness and isolation. I quickly went up, the sounds of anguish and pain faded away until it was completely quiet. I was now passing the Earth, it all happened so quickly. I arrived in a place facing some people that I was familiar with, but I didn't know how I knew them even though I felt like I'd known them forever. I could feel that they knew me and I could feel their love emanating through me, they were extremely happy to see me.

"I was still struggling to come to terms with my death and kept asking, 'What happened to Cindy.' I was worried about my body. They told me I was there with them and that's all that mattered."

After Cindy's salvation, her experience eventually ended when she decided she wanted to return to her body. What we know from positive experiences is that God is the light and the love, or Agape. Justin's experience told us that souls on Earth could not see the light for the dark. Our witnesses show us that souls that dwell in Hell are never truly alone and by calling on God, or in other cases, Jesus, they can be saved. However, it does appear to be a two-way deal, you must call for God or Jesus to be saved, this allows God or Jesus to reach into Hell and save us.

There is an exception to this, and this exception is the final piece to our puzzle. It is also one the most controversial subjects when it comes to NDE's. It is the subject of judgement and punishment.

I, Judge

Opinions on judgment and punishment vary depending on your religious beliefs, or lack of. For example, atheists and agnostics do not believe in judgement or punishment in the afterlife, because they do not believe in an afterlife.

For Christianity it is a little more complex. The Roman Catholic Church teaches Hell is eternal punishment for those that do not repent their sins, and people who lack communion with God. The Catholic Church also speaks of the destruction of souls. The Bible itself refers to Heaven and Hell frequently.

John 3:16 "For God so loved the world, that he gave his only begotten Son, that whosoever believeth in him should not perish, but have everlasting life."

Thessalonians 1:8–9 (NIV), "Those who do not know God and do not obey the gospel of our Lord Jesus, they will be punished with everlasting destruction and shut out from the presence of the Lord and from the glory of his might."

Judaism, on the other hand, has had a complex history as it relates to Heaven and Hell, going from a belief in the resurrection of the dead, through to no afterlife whatsoever. The closest concept Judaism has to Hell is Gehinnom. Unlike

Christianity's version of Hell, Gehinnom is not a permanent home for all of its residents. For the most wicked it is similar to Christianity, damning souls to torture for eternity. The less wicked suffer for a time in Hell before they are adequately punished, and then they just cease to exist. For the righteous, they go straight to 'Garden of Eden' where souls are trained for the 'World to Come'.

Islam is more aligned to Christianity as it relates to Hell, albeit with harsher criteria. In Islam being a non-believer or 'Shirk' is considered a grievous sin. Disobeying Islamic law and rejecting the messengers of Islam are also considered serious sins. Hell has various levels in the Islamic faith, in addition to raging fires, Islamic Hell also has a level of unbearable cold.

Hinduism shares similar traits with other mainstream religions. In Hinduism, Hell is called Naraka and has 28 levels, or separate Hells, which have specific punishments according to specific sins. Like Judaism, Naraka is not a permanent home for all of its residents. The big difference is what happens after a soul's punishment, in Hinduism the soul is reincarnated as a being according to their sins. The more severe the sin, the more mediocre the being the soul is reincarnated as.

When we look at the core religions in society, we find one consistent theme: Judgement. What we find overwhelmingly among both our positive and negative NDE, is that judgement is not passed by God, but by ourselves. This may be hard to fathom at first, why would anyone pass strict judgement on themselves? And even more unfathomable, why would anyone cast themselves down to Hell? This is a difficult question to answer, so instead of jumping straight into our interpretation, let us spend some time looking at what experiences our witnesses have brought back with them.

Life Review

We briefly covered the traditional view of judgement that religion teaches us, and even if the mechanics of Hell vary greatly among different religions, the concept of judgment is pretty consistent. Based on what we've discussed so far, it's difficult to reconcile an unconditionally loving God with a being that passes eternal damnation in a place we now know to be unimaginably horrific. This is even harder to accept if we consider the relatively low bar for sinners in modern times where secular society ranks third among all global religions.

I've tussled with many people on this subject, even my wife. For example, whilst not heavily religious, she has been brought up to believe Hell is eternal punishment, and that murderers, rapists, and the worst among us definitely and permanently end up in Hell. For her, any other interpretation of Hell or the idea that God does not judge and punish the guilty is irreconcilable, even offensive. This is a common belief system among even the 'slightly religious'.

Our witnesses describe to us in explicit detail how the process of judgement works, but only once have I read a witness account that connects this to Hell. We're going to look at that account shortly, but before we do, let's take a broader look at 'The Life Review'.

You may recall that none of our witness accounts have included any mention of the Life Review, whereas with positive experiences the Life Review occurs for most people. This indicates that the those who find themselves in Hell are never actually judged, which aligns with our interpretation of the Egregore of Hell. Remember that a person's own guilt, bitterness, or general negative emotional truth is what attracts them to Hell.

Frank

Frank fractured his skull during a car accident. During surgery Frank's experience began. Sometime into his experience, his life review began.

"The being then asked me to show what I had done with my life. I felt it was downloading all my experiences. I had no option because everything I had done was played in front of me."

Frank knows that his life's events are being 'downloaded'. The way in which a person's life experiences are presented to them varies greatly, Frank doesn't go into a great deal of detail, but we know his life is being played out in front of him. We'll see more examples of the various mechanisms our witnesses have experienced in the coming pages. Whilst we see free will in action during many witness experiences, the life review is not a choice. In all the reports of life reviews I've reviewed, no witness has ever been permitted to 'skip it'.

"My girlfriend at the time was going through a hard time and I couldn't give her the support she needed. I saw myself

walking out the door of the apartment. When I was gone, I saw her cry in torment. I could feel her pain and anguish. This made me angry and I cursed the light."

The key takeaway from Frank's experience is when he says, "I could feel her pain and anguish." For Frank, he felt anger when confronted with his girlfriend's feelings, but for others their emotions range from guilt, shame to intense apathy. Whilst this is clearly a distressing experience for Frank, imagine if he was experiencing something more sinister that he'd inflicted on someone else, such as murder or serious physical assault. Physical sensation is not the feeling that is relayed back to the experiencer, it is the emotional aspects of the experience. If you've ever been assaulted, you'll know how terrifying that experience is. We can only begin to imagine the fear and sadness for a victim of murder.

Raegan

Raegan suffered a horrible car accident which left the steering wheel impaled through her neck, whilst her passenger was thrown through the windscreen, making her a paraplegic for the rest of her life. During Raegan's experience, she entered into her Life Review.

"He stood beside me and directed me to look to my left, where I was replaying my life's less complimentary moments; I relived those moments and felt not only what I had done but also the hurt I had caused."

Again, we see our witness reliving the feelings and emotions of the people whose life Raegan has touched.

"Some of the things I would have never imagined could have caused pain. I was surprised that some things I may have worried about, like shoplifting a chocolate as a child, were not there whilst casual remarks which caused hurt unknown to me at the time were counted."

This is another common occurrence during the life review. Seemingly inconsequential events in our lives that we barely notice, are present throughout our life review.

We spoke about the importance of the force of love. How we treat people day to day is a part of that force. We can learn a lot from witnesses' life reviews. I have personally made a more concerted effort to show kindness to the people around me, to put myself in their shoes and to ask myself what I can do for others. It doesn't have to be as profound as saving a kitten from a burning building or building schools in Africa, that's just not practical. It can be simple gestures of kindness such as supporting those around you, making people feel better when their down, or giving food to a hungry homeless person. Whatever brings happiness and a smile to someone's face.

"When I became burdened with guilt, I was directed to other events which gave joy to others. Though I felt unworthy, it seemed the balance was in my favour. I received great Love."

Raegan didn't notice her casual hurtful remarks when they occurred, yet now she feels intense guilt.

Witnesses typically are more empathetic during and after their NDE than before they had their experience. As a result, when we go through our life review, we are more emotionally vulnerable to any negative emotions. This is important because we typically associate evil and cruel acts with people who lack empathy or compassion. A person's lack of empathy or compassion may well be a result of some underlying mental health condition, however, whatever mental problem a person has, it no longer exists once they pass over.

Others may have repressed their empathy and compassion through trauma or a broken upbringing. Whilst it is possible a person could carry this reduced sense of empathy and compassion to the other side, they would no less vulnerable to experiencing the negative emotions they have inflicted upon others as Reagan was.

Mohit

Mohit is from Iran and in 1977, at the age of 26, suffered serious injuries as the result of a head on car accident. Whilst he was in hospital, his body succumbed to his injuries and so began his journey to the other side.

Eventually Mohit arrived at his life review.

"I was showed a series of scenes that appeared in front of me like a movie. It was a movie of my life.

"Everything was in chronological order from the very beginning of my life on this Earth. There was a young woman with child. It was my mother and I was the child she was bearing. I became one with her body like a wave."

Many witnesses report experiencing their life as early as being a child in their mothers' womb. It is less about the physical reality of being an unborn baby, and more about the emotional experience. It's also symbolic in that it marks the beginning of our mortal journey.

"When I was a little kid, I was traveling in the car with my family by car and stopped in an open area. I was asked to go to a nearby river to collect some water. On my return the

weight of the bucket became too much for me. I decided to empty a little of the water. Instead of just pouring it into the ground, I saw a tree that on a dry patch of land. It looked lonely so I decided to pour the water on the roots of the tree. I waited until the water was absorbed into the ground around the tree. In this moment, the beings that accompanied me in my life review applauded me and felt such joy for such a simple act, it was like the universe was smiling. The beings comforting me were so proud of me. It was as though this was my biggest achievement of my life! This was peculiar to me, I didn't think this little act was such a big deal and believed I'd done far more important things. But I was told what I had done was incredibly important because I had done so purely from the heart, with absolutely no expectation of receiving anything back."

Random acts of kindness go unnoticed every day.

Many NDE witnesses report that these simple acts are vastly more important than creating a masterpiece or building a wonder. In Heaven we are measured on our acts of love and kindness. We spend so much time aspiring to be like to our idols or mimic their success, whether it's rockstars or movie legends, we believe the most important thing in our lives is to go big. But the reality is different than we might expect when it comes to how we are measured in Heaven, each of us can have an impact on the universe and humanity simply by showing love and kindness in everything we do. Mohit learns this simple act of kindness may well be the most important thing he's done in his life in the eyes of God. Made even more important due to the fact he did not expect anything in return,

Mohit simply acted instinctively to care for another life form without any expectation of reward.

Like most of us, Mohit is not perfect. There are events in his life where he has shown cruelty or contempt for others. Regardless of when these events occur, during our life review we will always endure in equal measure the emotional torment we have laid at the feet of others.

"When I was a 10-year-old boy, I bullied a boy at school about the same age as me. I would attack him and beat him without mercy. I could now feel his intense pain, he was tortured inside and would cry on his way home from school. The negative energy he radiated from his pain and suffering was being absorbed by everything around him, the tree's, the bird's and even the flies were affected by it. I felt all the pain and hurt I had inflicted on him, I saw how it affected his parents when they worried every time they saw him off to school and when he was a few minutes late returning from home."

Mohit illustrates that how we treat each other ripples through everything and everyone. Just as our other witness's experienced, when it comes to our life review, we cannot escape the cruelty and pain we have inflicted on others. In Mohit's statement he mentions how the birds and the flies were affected, but importantly, he also felt the torment of his victim's parents.

Imagine this scenario for someone as evil as Hitler. Imagine the countless lives his actions directly impacted. The anguish and pain that resulted from his actions condensed into a single experience would no doubt be immeasurably painful.

We'll soon cover what happens when one cannot endure their life review.

But as our next witness explains, it is not God that judges us, it is ourselves.

Anthony

In 1989 Anthony had a critical accident whilst at a school function. He was alone when through a series of unfortunate accidents, he had hung himself. We join Anthony's experience at the moment he starts his life review.

"I was brought to a large room and in the centre, there was a table with a dome hovering over it. I looked into the dome and my life review began. I experienced my life from many different perspectives. I could feel what others felt from my actions. It was difficult to get through, but I understood it was important that I learnt and grew from my life on Earth. I relived people laughing and crying because of the things I'd do on Earth."

For Mohit it was a movie, for Anthony he looks into a dome to experience his life review. Like our other witnesses, Anthony finds it hard to live through the pain and suffering he has caused others.

"My spirit guide assured me it was okay, that we are all loved; that this was not a judgment. I was told that we learn best by experiencing things for ourselves. God is not judging

us. Our purpose is to learn. The most difficult part comes from seeing so many different people's perspectives and experiencing their pain."

Anthony is assured that God is not judging him, but that does not mean we are not being judged. We are judging ourselves. As we have already discussed our empathy and compassion is heightened in the afterlife, we are not weighed down but our negative mortal traits. We are in a place of unconditional love and acceptance surrounded by beings that love us as if they have known us our entire existence. Even though we are comforted during this process, in this perfect environment of unconditional acceptance and love it must be difficult to share moments of our lives where we have showed cruelty and inflicted pain on others.

So far, we have reviewed testimonies where our witnesses, whilst difficult, have successfully completed their life reviews. But what happens when we are unable to suffer the pain we have inflicted upon others? Can we just cancel our life review and make our way into Heaven? Are we punished, and if so, who punishes us, is it God?

Augustus

When it comes to God and the afterlife, we are accustomed to biblical and ancient records. All of the NDE's we've reviewed so far occurred in the twentieth and twenty-first century. In reality NDE's go back much further. The world became a much bigger place as recently as the mid-twentieth century, so it is not surprising there are few recorded NDE's going back much further.

In 696 AD Augustus suffered from a sickness that escalated daily until he died one evening at dusk. In the morning he came to life and suddenly sat up where all those who sat beside him fled in terror, only his wife who loved him dearly, although trembling and afraid, remained with him. He comforted her saying:

"Fear not, for I am now in very deed risen from death whereof I was holden, and permitted again to live among men; nevertheless, hereafter I must not live as I was wont, but after a very different manner."

There are many parts of Augustus's experience that align with those of our witnesses in modern times. We have covered extensively the mode of communication in the afterlife.

Augustus confirms this in his own account. He also speaks to the great light of Heaven exceeding the brightness of the sun.

"So great was the light shed over all this place that it seemed to exceed the brightness of the day, or the rays of the noontide sun.

"In this field were innumerable companies of men clothed in white, and many seats of rejoicing multitudes. As he led me through the midst of bands of happy inhabitants, I began to think that this perchance might be the kingdom of Heaven, of which I had often heard tell. He answered to my thought, saying, 'Nay, this is not the kingdom of Heaven, as you think.'"

During Augustus's journey he is shown a vision of Hell, again, his account aligns with witness testimony from modern times.

"Now whereas an innumerable multitude of misshapen spirits were thus tormented far and near with this interchange of misery, as far as I could see, without any interval of rest, I began to think that peradventure this might be Hell, of whose intolerable torments I had often heard men talk. My guide, who went before me, answered to my thought, saying, 'Think not so, for this is not the Hell you believe it to be.'

"Moreover, a stench, foul beyond compare, burst forth with the vapours, and filled all those dark places. Having stood there a long time in much dread, not knowing what to do, which way to turn, or what end awaited me, on a sudden I heard behind me the sound of a mighty and miserable lamentation, and at the same time noisy laughter, as of a rude

multitude insulting captured enemies. When that noise, growing plainer, came up to me, I beheld a crowd of evil spirits dragging five souls of men, wailing and shrieking, into the midst of the darkness, whilst they themselves exulted and laughed."

Augustus observes the laughing and mocking we have covered in other witness accounts. He also speaks of the foul stench, another common theme when describing Hell. He now finds himself among the tormented, at this moment he calls for his saviour. It's important to remember your every thought is heard in the afterlife, thinking something is the same as saying it.

"Being thus on all sides encompassed with enemies and shades of darkness, and casting my eyes hither and thither if haply anywhere help might be found whereby I might be saved, there appeared behind me, on the way by which I had come, as it were, the brightness of a star shining amidst the darkness; which waxing greater by degrees, came rapidly towards me: and when it drew near, all those evil spirits, that sought to carry me away with their tongs, dispersed and fled."

As with our other witnesses, Augustus sees a light in the darkness which grows stronger as it approaches, eventually causing the evil beings around him to flee. His savour asks him if he understands what he has seen.

" 'Do you know what all these things are which you have seen?' I answered, 'No,' and then he said, 'That valley which you beheld terrible with flaming fire and freezing cold, is the

place in which the souls of those are tried and punished, who, delaying to confess and amend their crimes, at length have recourse to repentance at the point of death, and so go forth from the body; but nevertheless because they, even at their death, confessed and repented, they shall all be received into the kingdom of Heaven at the day of judgment."

What we can take from Augustus's newfound knowledge is that souls can repent even at the point of death. It's important we don't take Augustus's words too literally. Augustus was a religious man where soon after coming back to the life he went on to live in a monastery in England until his death. He routinely shared his stories with King Alfred. This was a time in England when religion was a way of life for most of the population. Because of this, it is possible his story was embellished to serve religious doctrine.

What Augustus's story tells us is that we can repent for our actions in life at the time of death instead of only having the opportunity to repent in life. Based on the witness statements featured in this book, and thousands of other NDE experiences, we can surmise that the moment of judgement is the life review. But it is not judgment in the biblical sense of the word. It's easy to associate the word 'repent' with some religious act when in fact it just means 'feel or express sincere regret or remorse about one's wrongdoing or sin', in other words feeling regret for wrongdoing.

It's now time to look at what happens when a person does not want to complete their life review. We are all given the opportunity to review our lives when we pass over. We know we are not being judged by God but knowing this may make it harder to forgive ourselves.

Knowing that God forgives us no matter what can result in us feeling even less worthy of his love, and we already know what happens when we believe we truly and deeply do not deserve Heaven or God's love.

Jacob

In 1989 Jacob was a young 19-year-old arrogant teenager, by his own words. When his long-term girlfriend ended their relationship, Jacob could not handle the rejection and in a moment of grief and madness, he washed down several bottles of drugs with a bottle of Rum. Jacob passed away on his way to the hospital.

"I was being shown visions of all the horrible things I had done in my life, I was being put into other people's minds as I was doing bad things to them. I felt how insensitive I had been to people and didn't even realise it. It was agonising and crushing to relive these things I had forgotten about or didn't care about at the time. I was made to feel the way I made others feel. The pain became too overwhelming and so I closed my eyes.

"Suddenly I was somewhere else. I opened my tear-soaked eyes and found myself crouched in a cave of some variety. The ceilings were low, and the floor was wet and cold, it was almost pitch black and was very dark. I felt abandoned and alone. I tried to move in the cave, but I couldn't crawl without getting soaking wet and there was no way I could stand because the ceiling was so low. I saw a faint light

ahead; I was hopeful the light would warm me. As I shuffled through the low cave I came to an opening, inside I could see the light from flames flickering around the mouth of the entrance.

"There were people sitting crouched around the entrance of this cave. I asked them where I was, and they told me to be silent otherwise I would be next. Then a huge monstrous demon emerged from the cave and dragged a group of them inside kicking and screaming. I feared I would be next, so I curled up and closed my eyes. When I closed my eyes, I was again overwhelmed with visions and feelings of all the bad things I've done in my life. When I opened my eyes, I was back at this cave entrance awaiting my horrible fate. I now realised that I could not close my eyes without confronting the actions of my life. I looked at the other people outside the cave entrance and noticed they all looked exhausted and then realised it's because they too could not close their eyes and face their own actions in life."

In 696 AD Augustus was told, *"That valley which you beheld terrible with flaming fire and freezing cold, is the place in which the souls of those are tried and punished, who, delaying to confess and amend their crimes."* Here we find that Jacob is unable to face the wrongs of his life. We could say that Jacob is 'delaying to confess and amend his crimes'. Jacob was not judged by God, he chose this fate because he refuses to face and learn from the actions of his life. It would also appear that those in Jacob's company also cannot face the choices they made in their lives, and how this has affected other people. Jacob and the people he shares this terrible experience with need simply close their eyes and experience the wrongs they have bestowed upon others to escape this fiery Hell. So, Jacob has a choice: face your life and the ways you have affected others or remain in this Hell until you do so.

"I don't know how long it was, but it was a long time when my eyes began to burn from keeping them open, I eventually decided that it was worth putting up with the suffering I had caused others. I knew it would soon be over if I could just close my eyes for a while. I cried quietly as the feelings and scenes of my evil acts flooded my mind.

"The screaming and the visions of what I'd done stopped. It was now silent."

Jacob faced his actions on Earth and was spared Hell, his experience continues in a positive fashion until he is revived by doctors.

We know that Jacob did not commit any serious crimes in his life. The evil acts he refers to relate to the way he has treated others, with insensitivity and contempt.

Despite this, Jacob is initially unable to face his actions. The other poor souls he encountered by the cave also could not face their actions in life, and so they too found themselves in Hell.

Penance

The subject of judgement and punishment is a hot topic for millions, if not billions of people. For the religious among us the general concept is that we are judged and punished by God when it's our time to leave this mortal life. As we've already discussed, this process normally involves Hell or some kind of underworld. For people that have some form of a belief system but are not actively practising a specific religion, the concept of judgement, punishment, Heaven and Hell is relatively common. Personally, I know more people that fall into the latter category than the former.

We expect people with strong religious beliefs to align with the teachings of their chosen doctrine as it relates to judgment and punishment, but surprisingly, I've personally found the subject of judgment and punishment is emotive even for people with limited religious beliefs. As I mentioned earlier, my wife was offended at the idea that God does not send the evil and cruel among us to Hell.

It's now time to take everything we've learnt from our witnesses and come up with a digestible interpretation. We've already discussed that our souls have a heightened sense of compassion and empathy. This combined with experiencing the pain and suffering we have caused others must be overwhelming when we are going through our life review, as we witnessed with Jacob. Jacob himself confessed to having little empathy for his actions when he committed them, but he was unable to process his actions and how they affected other people during his life review. Despite the Hell he found himself in, Jacob still struggled to complete his life review.

But if it is not God judging us for these actions, then why did Jacob end up in Hell, as momentary as it was?

Remember the Egregore? It attracts negative energy from all the souls that inhabit it forming a perpetual Hell of our darkest feelings and thoughts. We spoke about how there is no place in Heaven for negative human emotion. All things evil, as much as we try to blame them on mythical creatures such as the Devil, are human creations.

We cannot enter Heaven when we are literally weighed down by these negative emotions, or evil. This was never our natural state. It would be like an oil slick consuming the most beautiful ocean. Our natural state as souls is pure love, or Agape. A corrupted soul is simply not compatible with Heaven. We come to Earth to enrich our souls, to learn how to love, to show compassion and empathy, in an environment often seeped in evil and greed.

When we finally pass over to the other side, it's essential we review our lives and learn from our actions, otherwise our entire lives give nothing to eternal divine growth. During the life review, as we learn from our mistakes in life, we shed the negative energy and emotion associated to these acts, no matter how evil they are. We repent one final time.

It's important to understand this process is not punishment. As we've already discussed, acts of love and kindness are celebrated with immense joy. Once we have freed ourselves from our negative human energy, we can pass into Heaven, where we are all very much wanted.

But for those that cannot shed their negative energy, which is intrinsically weaved into their soul until they complete their life review, they cannot complete their journey to Heaven. It is their choice, they have chosen not to learn from the deeds and actions of their life, as painful and distressing as that may be. This negative energy, or evil, needs to go somewhere. The person that carries this evil energy cannot go to Heaven, so where will they go?

They go where all negative energy goes; they go to Hell. Not because they deserve it, not because God sent them there, not because of the severity of their crimes, they go there because they cannot, or will not, shed themselves of their negative energy caused by their own actions, and therefore they keep themselves out of Heaven.

Just as Jacob experienced, he could at any time close his eyes and complete his life review, thereby returning to Heaven, which is exactly what he did. His negative acts in life were arrogance, contempt, and indifference to others. Imagine now for a moment the sheer agony for someone such as Hitler who murdered six million Jews during the second world war, or Vlad the Impaler who left a forest of 20,000 impaled men, woman and children in a single invasion of an Ottoman village.

During their life review they would not only have to feel the fear and anguish of every one of their victims, but also the pain and anguish of the friends and families that were left behind to pick up the pieces. They would live the experience of every single person affected by their acts of hatred.

If Jacob struggled to face his comparatively minor transgressions against other people in his life, do you think the likes of Hitler and Vlad could endure such a thing? Any lack of remorse they carried in their human body, related to mental health for example, would no longer exist in their spiritual form. They would recover their empathy and compassion they lacked in life, because in death it is the natural state of all of our souls. Even if they could endure such an experience, I would argue that this alone is a Hell of its own. If they were unable to get through their life review, which is likely, they would find themselves in the Egregore of Hell, because they have not shed themselves of their negative energy and therefore by the law of attraction, they would be 'sucked' into Hell, a term we've heard used often by our witnesses.

In summary, whilst it may be a difficult experience to get through if you've lived a life of cruelty and contempt, making it through our life review is still our decision. At any time, if we find ourselves in Hell, we can return to Heaven simply by completing our life review.

This will be harder for some more than others, but it is an essential part of our existence, and our lives on Earth.

Unfortunately, Jacob's experience is the only one I've come across where someone was unable to complete their life review, and as a result ended up in Hell. However, there are many examples of witnesses struggling with their life review.

"After choosing to return to my earthly body, I had to review all of my actions that were unkind towards others. Because of my religious upbringing, I always believed that when we die, we would be punished.

"Unfortunately, I was just never sure about the severity of what wrong meant in Heaven's terms. Contrary to my belief system, the light never judged me. I was made to judge myself. Another important part to my life's review demanded that I feel the same emotional pain others felt whenever I hurt their feeling with actions or words. By seeing other people's hearts and knowing how they were affected, it caused me to feel remorseful and ashamed.

Thankfully, after the experience ended, the light granted me the understanding I needed, and my soul found forgiveness." – Calvin, 1997

"God then showed me all my life from birth until NDE. I felt and experienced again all these events and I also felt emotions I had raised in others. I was my only judge! This experience was very painful. I dare not imagine what Adolf Hitler underwent when feeling the pain of millions of individuals. God showed me when I had generously done things without thinking about it beforehand, and when I had done unloving things. I even saw myself stealing sweets in a shop, thinking to myself, 'Whew, nobody saw me!' Indeed, somebody saw me. Yes, God saw me! But he does not judge me. In fact, this is what hit me the most. God does not judge, he just loves us with unconditional love, this love is indescribable, it is not like what we feel on earth, this is rather a force-of-love." – Liam, 2009

"This time, my life flashed before me. Whole years of my life flashed by in a second, but with complete clarity. Time had no meaning here. Even more dramatic, decisions I had made in a split second were played back to me. I understood

not only the impact they had made in my life, but the impact on countless other lives as well. Some decisions I was proud of, while some I lowered my eyes in humiliation and shame. Yet, there was no judgment, other than my own." – Lee, 2018

"At another point closer to the beginning I think, I was in a court setting for my life review. I was shown what happened to me, my life, my sins, my love, and forgiveness of others by me. I cried for my sins, my shame, and my repentance. I was very shameful, mortified and sorry." – John, 1969

We see some consistent themes in our witness accounts. Liam, Lee, and Calvin confirm that God is not judging us, we are judging ourselves, whilst both John and Lee speak of the shame they felt from their review.

Perhaps this is the judgement scripture speaks of, the life review. It's entirely fair to position the life review as penance, but it is penance to ourselves. Our time on Earth is our opportunity to learn, grow and enrich our souls. We teach our souls that in the face of tragic loss and suffering we become the best, most compassionate, loving versions of ourselves. We learn how important it is for us to care for each other and that we are one people, no matter what part of this tiny planet we inhabit, what language we speak, or how we happen to look. Let's take another look at what Augustus's guide told him during his experience in 696 AD.

'That valley which you beheld terrible with flaming fire and freezing cold, is the place in which the souls of those are tried and punished, who, delaying to confess and amend their crimes, at length have recourse to repentance at the point of death, and so go forth from the body; but nevertheless,

because they, even at their death, confessed and repented, they shall all be received into the kingdom of Heaven at the day of judgment."

Augustus's guide refers to the life review as a process of being tried and punished. This is a medieval interpretation of the process no doubt verbalised in such a way that Augustus could understand it. His guide continues *'delaying to confess and amend their crimes, at length have recourse to repentance at the point of death'*. Remember how Jacob could not complete his life review? In 696AD we could say he was *'delaying to confess and amend his crimes'*, this is the same as not completing your life review. We also know from Jacob he could repent at any time by simply closing his eyes and completing his life review, he has *'recourse to repentance'* at the point of death.

Augustus's guide also specifically says *'at length have recourse to repentance'*. We can interpret this as souls having as much time as they need to complete their life review and forgive themselves.

The final statement, *'but nevertheless, because they, even at their death, confessed and repented, they shall all be received into the kingdom of Heaven at the day of judgment'* tells us that once we complete our life review, or repent in medieval terms, we can enter the kingdom of Heaven, even after death.

For many people, this information may provide some comfort if you feel strongly that people who commit evil acts in life should be punished in death. I doubt I'm the only person that has watched the daily news in horror as a news anchor reports of a horrible crime against an innocent person, wishing that the perpetrator would somehow have to suffer through the pain they inflicted on their victim. It does seem a fitting punishment that perpetrators of evil will one day have to suffer through that which they have inflicted on other people. But regardless of our own personal feelings as it relates to crime and punishment, the intent of the life review is not to punish people. It's intended to enrich their souls and help them learn the value of compassion, kindness, and love. The way in which we learn these essential qualities is through understanding the suffering we have imposed on others, and what we could have done differently.

The life review is not a one-sided evaluation of our lives, where we only see the negative aspects of our time on Earth, we also focus on our accomplishments. These accomplishments are not what you might expect, it's not graduation, building a monument or creating an artistic masterpiece. The most celebrated accomplishments are the ones you probably didn't even notice in life. For example, Mohit stopped to water a dry tree, he did this instinctively, he didn't do it because he expected some kind of reward or praise. Any act of kindness, compassion or empathy is celebrated during the life review, as long as you're not doing it for your own personal gain. When I say personal gain, I mean for money or greed. It's really not that complicated, we all know the difference between kindness and cruelty, between selfishness and selflessness.

As a human, you may never accept that ALL are forgiven by God, no matter what evils they commit. Can I honestly say that if someone hurt or killed my son, I could forgive them? No, I don't think I could. That doesn't change the fact that I know this is what God wants from me. I am imperfect, I am only human. But there are those that can, and have, forgiven such evils. We have all seen mothers and fathers forgive the murderers of their children on the news. These exceptional examples of humanity are usually religious people with strong values. Forgiveness sometimes benefits the offender, but usually it's the victim or the families that benefit the most from forgiveness.

The School of Life

In the 2007 movie *Evan Almighty*, Morgan Freeman's character said:

> *"If someone prays for patience, you think God gives them patience? Or does he give them the opportunity to be patient? If he prayed for courage, does God give him courage, or does he give him opportunities to be courageous? If he prayed for the family to be closer, do you think God zaps them with warm fuzzy feelings, or does he give them the opportunities to love each other?"*

This simple statement sums up many of the reasons why we're here on Earth. Simply having things handed to us on a plate doesn't teach us the value of things, or more importantly the value of each other. This applies more to our emotional and spiritual growth than our ability to grow as productive individuals in society. Our ability to socialise and be productive members of society is of course important to our earthbound existence, but not so much in Heaven.

There are two tangible things we take with us when we die, our consciousness (or who we are) and our knowledge. We've already established we gain instant understanding and universal knowledge when we take our last breath in our earthly vessels. It's unlikely there is any knowledge we can take with us that isn't already known in the heavenly realm.

There are, however, many things we cannot learn in Heaven, things we can only learn during our short lives on this tiny blue marble. Overcoming or supporting someone with Heroin addiction, giving our last $10 to someone in need, comforting someone facing a painful and difficult situation in their lives, or simply making someone feel better about themselves when they are at their lowest.

There are also personal struggles we can learn from. Overcoming hate and choosing unity, overcoming addiction, and choosing life, rejecting cruelty and choosing kindness. God does not expect you to be an angel, what could you possibly learn from this on Earth that you couldn't learn in Heaven?

What God wants from us, but does not demand, is that we treat each other with kindness, empathy, compassion, and most of all, love. Free will is a fickle thing, part of your journey in life, your mission, is entirely dictated by your free will. If you did not have free will, how would you learn? In business we have many mottos around mistakes and failure. For example, "Fail fast and fail often," and "Success is normally found in a pile of mistakes." Our world's greatest philosophers and historic figures also recognise the importance of mistakes. Albert Einstein said, "A person who never made a mistake never tried anything new." Elbert Hubbard said, "The greatest mistake a man can ever make is to be afraid of making one." Adam Osborne said, "The most valuable thing you can make is a mistake – you can't learn anything from being perfect." I've made plenty of grade A mistakes, but I've learnt from them all, and they've made me a better, stronger person. It's okay to make mistakes, and it's okay to mess things up, what's important is that you learn from these mistakes. This includes anything from showing contempt to a stranger, heinous acts of evil and cruelty, to self-inflicted harm. Of course, many people pass over without learning anything about compassion, kindness, and love. For them, their life review will be extensive and difficult, but like everyone else they will be given the opportunity to learn and forgive themselves.

Many of our witnesses, during their NDE's, become aware that our purpose in life is to learn. Cabell suffered critical illness in hospital in 1976, leading to a cessation of breathing which led to his NDE. Just like most witnesses, he is imparted with knowledge on the meaning of life.

"The experience was not of the mind but what I believe to be of the soul and spirit. There was a huge light and my soul was at a learning point, our lives spent here in body, and soul being present in them, is to learn as much as we can."

In 2001 Gina accidentally overdosed on drugs leading to her NDE. After recovering from her NDE, she recalls every detail of her experience, except for one thing.

"When I opened my eyes, it was gone. I was lying there trying to remember. My mind could remember every scene of what happened, but not that one most important thing. I felt like I was not allowed to have that knowledge here, like, if we knew, we wouldn't learn what we needed to learn. Life is a school, nothing more."

The important thing Gina cannot remember is commonly taken away from the memory of witnesses, and we've discussed this a few times. Knowledge of the future is always redacted from our witness's memories. As Gina said, if we knew, we wouldn't learn what we need to.

In 1964, Terry suffocated from drowning whilst learning to swim as a child.

"Then I remember experiencing everything I had done in my entire life with some kind of explanation of what had been done well and what I could have done differently. This part did not frighten me at all and was accompanied by a total lack of judgment, and a sensation of being totally accepted and cared for.

"I felt I was guided in this explanation by a presence who simply wanted me to learn from my life, about how I could be a better person in the future."

Terry reinforces the purpose of the life review, to learn, not to be judged. During the life review, empathy and compassion are the vessels for this learning. By experiencing what we have done to others, we are seeing it entirely from their perspective. Any preconceptions we have, any lifelong hatred we harbour that we think justifies our acts of cruelness, are not present in the victims of our cruelty. We see and experience our actions from a completely different perspective.

Are You Going to Hell?

And so, we conclude this book and ask ourselves that burning question, are you going to Hell? I hope by now you understand that Hell is not yours, or anyone else's destiny. The decision to descend into the depths of Hell is entirely your own, made either at the time of death or during your life review. Of course, you would not consciously make the decision to commit yourself to Hell. Anastasia's story illustrates this best when she said, *"I stayed like this for a while and then all of a sudden my negative past consumed me. I hadn't dealt with the trauma and pain of my past; I was overwhelmed by it. All the guilt, pain and suppressed anger flowed back into my heart, but it was amplified and saturated me. I felt as though I did not deserve what I just experienced, I didn't deserve all that peace, all I had in my mind were nasty negative thoughts about myself. I reverted to my life long natural state of crippling depression."* It was precisely this moment that Anastasia found herself in Hell, she didn't consciously decide to go to Hell, it was her emotional truth that attracted her there.

I've asked myself many times during the course of my research and writing this book, "Will I go to Hell?" As I mentioned at the beginning of this book, I never had an NDE, despite my regular brushes with critical illness. Was it because Heaven was closed to me, and Hell would be my ultimate destination? When I started out, I wasn't sure.

Then I started to look back through my life and found plenty of times where I would be ashamed of my actions, particularly in the presence of God, or the overwhelming love and compassion of Agape. In fact, I only had to go back less than a year to find a situation where I'd shown contempt or indifference for someone's feelings. I'm not an outwardly aggressive person, even during my early years among gangsters and drug dealers, I've never been an aggressive person. But again, I'm only human, and as a result I had become angry, and could become intimidatingly direct if I get upset. In recent memory I could confidently say that every situation where I have become this direct, has been because someone was either being offensive to me or trying to antagonise me. But that's no excuse when my time comes. Whether I believe it was deserved or not, being cruel is being cruel. Forgiveness is one of the key lessons we're given the opportunity to learn during our time on Earth. Instead of being combative, I could have chosen to employ understanding and forgiveness. It is sometimes the hardest lesson to learn because the need for us to forgive someone implies we've been wronged in some way. Continuing with this thought exercise I went back even further, all the way to my teenage years. Throughout my life there are many times when I have treated people without empathy or compassion, where I've chosen myself at the detriment to others. Taking everything that's happened to me throughout my life, all my acts of contempt and anger, I do not believe my guilt, shame, or indifference will attract me to Hell. I am at my core an empathetic and compassionate person.

And then I asked myself the question, can I learn from my mistakes during my lifetime, so I don't have to face these heart wrenching events during my life review? I think it is possible. Whilst our witnesses wouldn't know that some negative aspects of their life were not featured in their life review, there are cases where witnesses have reported an entirely positive life review, despite being aware of some acts of contempt or hatred during their lifetime. This tells us that these witnesses learnt what they needed to learn during their lives, and therefore didn't need to review them during their life review. If you think about it, learning to be a better person during our lives is preferable to learning how to be a better person in death, during our life review. If we learn how to better people in life, we can go on to practice our new wisdom enriching the lives of those around us. This thought exercise will also help you to identify times in your life, which you may have dismissed at the time, where you've treated others cruelly, or with contempt. You might be surprised at what you recall.

I've mentioned many times over that there is no judgement in Heaven, at least not from a divine perspective. But you could be forgiven for interpreting the life review as a form of punishment. The key difference between the life review, and the judgement that mainstream religions teach, is what God wants from us. In religion there is a lot of focus on how you should behave, and a laundry list of things that God 'expects' from you. For example, "Deuteronomy 22:5 ESV / 83", "*A woman shall not wear a man's garment, nor shall a man put on a woman's cloak, for whoever does these things is an abomination to the Lord your God.*" I don' think God cares what you wear, he only cares how you treat others. He does not care who you love, only that you loved. "Ecclesiastes 3:1-10", "*For everything there is a season, and a time for every matter under heaven: a time to be born, and a time to die; a time to plant, and a time to pluck up what is planted; a time to kill, and a time to heal…*" This is not rocket science, killing people is not an act of love, kindness, compassion, or empathy. The fact that so many religions teach, or are interpreted as, justifying murder for some ideological belief is baffling to me. How can we call ourselves civilised if we think murdering people is acceptable? I'm not suggesting that nations should not defend themselves, or people should not protect themselves. The life review is not a process of checking boxes. God is the most intelligent being in all of existence, I personally think he'll understand if people have no choice to end someone's life, to preserve their own, or to defend others.

Overall, most religions teach love, kindness, forgiveness, and compassion. But many also teach division, taking the focus away from treating everyone with love and compassion, to only treating those that share our ideological beliefs with kindness and love. Our witnesses tell a different story. If I was going to surmise everything we've learnt in this book as it relates to how we live our lives, I would say God expects the following things from us. Treat others with kindness, love, compassion, and empathy. Choose love over hate, know I am always here for and with you, and just have fun. That's it, it's that simple. For anything else, just ask yourself, am I doing this out of kindness, understanding and compassion, or am I doing this out of hate, anger, greed, or contempt. I know it must seem like I'm bashing religion, I'm not, I'm simply trying to demonstrate that God cares about you, and loves you, no matter what you believe. We should always choose unity over division. Anything that teaches division is not God's work. However, anything that teaches love, compassion and kindness is God's work. Ultimately, most religions balance out in favour of love, which makes them an essential part of society. That being said, the world is filled with kind, compassionate and loving people who practice no religion whatsoever, and whether they believe it or not, they too will ultimately reside in Heaven.

At the time of writing this book we are going through a global pandemic, social division, and political upheaval. People are more willing to hurt others based on their ideological beliefs, be it religious or political.

My advice, look back at your life right now, ask yourself, "Have I treated others the way I would want to be treated?" If not, why not? And what can you change now? When you feel anger and contempt bubbling up, think to yourself, what if that was my mother, my child, my brother, my wife, my husband, or anyone that you love. A couple of weeks ago I became angry at indecisive driver. I took a moment to try and see things from their point of view. I managed to catch sight of the person driving, it was a woman. She had children in the car. As I further analysed the situation, I realised she was stressed, I suspect she wasn't sure how to get where she was going, and as a result of her stress, she was making mistakes. I then remembered this is exactly how my own mother used to drive. It broke my heart to think that anyone could be directing the same contempt I felt at that moment, toward my own mother. A wonderful woman, loving, compassionate and quite the opposite of angry or cruel. I immediately calmed down, and instead started to think, how could I help this woman?

It is these simple things In our lives that we can start to change to train ourselves to be more compassionate and caring in everything we do. Don't forget, your acts of kindness ripple through the universe.

But most importantly of all, you have to forgive yourself. Life is hard, you're going to make mistakes and people are going to get hurt, including you. Just learn from these things. When you do something you believe is cruel or evil, take a moment to figure out how you could have done things differently, learn from it, forgive yourself and move on. Life is a marathon, not a sprint. It is literally never to late to learn and it's certainly never to late to forgive yourself. The fact we are even here walking around in these fragile bodies is a testament to our courage.

The End

I want to wrap up one last loose end. Why didn't I have an NDE during my brushes with near death? We already discussed the importance of this question to researchers.

The general consensus is that NDE's occur to people that need them. I believe this is the reason I never had an NDE, because I didn't need the experience in order to walk the path that's been laid out in front of me. If I look at how my life eventually worked out, it was the people around that me that taught me the lessons I needed and showed me the kindness and compassion that steered my ship.

The second question that led me to writing these pages, am I going to Hell? No, I do not think I am. Not because I'm a God-fearing person, not because I've never hurt anyone or committed a sin. It's because looking back at my life, I felt remorse for the wrongs I have done, I then forgave myself for these things. If I ever face the same or similar circumstances again, I will choose a different path, I will not make the same mistake. In addition to this I work everyday to better myself, to turn away from anger and hate, and instead try to forgive and support those around me. Sometimes I do a good job, other times not so much.

But it's nothing I, or you, can't work on.

Filling these pages has been a pleasure, and I hope you have the same experience reading them. I know it's a lot to digest, and I encourage you to do your own research. You can find thousands of NDE accounts at NDERF here: http://www.nderf.org. If just one person evades the horror and torment of Hell, or chooses kindness over cruelty, then it was worth writing this book.

Before I write the final sentence in this book, I want to leave you with a cliff-hanger to ponder until we meet again. You chose to be here, you chose the life you are leading, you made a deal with God.

Until we meet again, take care of yourselves, and each other...

Your friend, David.